CoffeeScript

Accelerated JavaScript Development,
Second Edition

Trevor Burnham

The Pragmatic Bookshelf

Dallas, Texas • Raleigh, North Carolina

Many of the designations used by manufacturers and sellers to distinguish their products are claimed as trademarks. Where those designations appear in this book, and The Pragmatic Programmers, LLC was aware of a trademark claim, the designations have been printed in initial capital letters or in all capitals. The Pragmatic Starter Kit, The Pragmatic Programmer, Pragmatic Programming, Pragmatic Bookshelf, PragProg and the linking g device are trademarks of The Pragmatic Programmers, LLC.

Every precaution was taken in the preparation of this book. However, the publisher assumes no responsibility for errors or omissions, or for damages that may result from the use of information (including program listings) contained herein.

Our Pragmatic courses, workshops, and other products can help you and your team create better software and have more fun. For more information, as well as the latest Pragmatic titles, please visit us at *https://pragprog.com*.

The team that produced this book includes:

Michael Swaine (editor)
Potomac Indexing (indexer)
Cathleen Small (copyeditor)
Dave Thomas (typesetter)
Janet Furlow (producer)
Ellie Callahan (support)

For international rights, please contact *rights@pragprog.com*.

Printed in the United States of America.
ISBN-13: 978-1-94122-226-3
Printed on acid-free paper.
Book version: P1.0—February 2015

Contents

Foreword

JavaScript was born free, but until recently it was in chains everywhere.

JavaScript wasn't always a very pleasant language to work in: it's terribly slow, it's implemented with different quirks in different browsers, and it's been stuck fast in the amber of time since the late 1990s. Perhaps you used it in the past to implement a drop-down menu or a reorderable list, but you probably didn't enjoy the experience.

Fortunately for us, the JavaScript of today is enjoying a well-deserved renaissance. Thanks to the tireless efforts of browser implementers, JavaScript is now the fastest mainstream dynamic language. It's present everywhere, from servers to Photoshop, and it's the only language you can use to program all angles of the Web.

CoffeeScript is a little language that aims to give you easy access to the good parts of JavaScript: the first-class functions, the hash-like objects, even the much-misunderstood prototype chain. If we do our job right, you'll end up writing one-third less code to generate much the same JavaScript you would've written in the first place.

CoffeeScript places a high value on the readability of code and the elimination of syntactic clutter. At the same time, there's a fairly one-to-one correspondence between CoffeeScript and JavaScript, which means that there should be no performance penalty—in fact, many JavaScript libraries end up running faster after being ported to CoffeeScript, due to some of the optimizations the compiler can perform.

You're fortunate to have picked up this book, because Trevor has been an enthusiastic contributor to CoffeeScript since the early days. Few people know more about the ins and outs of the language or the history of the debate behind language features and omissions than he does. This book is a gentle introduction to CoffeeScript led by an expert guide.

I'm looking forward to hearing about all of the exciting projects that I'm sure will come out of it, and—who knows—perhaps you'll be inspired to create a little language of your very own.

Jeremy Ashkenas, creator of CoffeeScript

April 2011

Acknowledgments

My warmest thanks to Jeremy Ashkenas for creating the CoffeeScript language and serving as its steward for all these years. No one better embodies the hacker ethos: the curiosity to try new things, the drive to see them through, and the generosity to share the results with the world. Thanks also to Coffee-Script's other contributors, who are too numerous to name here.[1]

Thanks to the technical reviewers and beta readers who provided valuable feedback for this edition: Vincent Bray, Javier Collado, Matthew Critchlow, Daniel Lamb, Rod Hilton, Scott Leberknight, Staphany Park, and Travis Swicegood.

Some thanks from the first edition bear repeating. I'd like to thank technical reviewers Javier Collado, Kevin Gisi, Darcy Laycock, Scott Leberknight, Sam Stephenson, Travis Swicegood, Federico Tomassetti, Stefan Turalski, and Dr. Nic Williams. Special thanks to experts Jeremy Ashkenas, Brendan Eich, and Michael Ficarra for their assistance.

Thanks to the Pragmatic Bookshelf for taking a chance all those years ago on a proposal from an unknown writer about a then-obscure language, and special thanks to the team that helped me produce this second edition. First and foremost to editor Michael Swaine, without whom I don't know how I would have finished this. Thanks also to managing editor Susannah Pfalzer and to the Prags themselves, Dave Thomas and Andy Hunt.

Thanks to my employer, HubSpot, for allowing me all the time I asked for to work on this edition. And for Panini Club.

Thanks, finally, to my parents, Scott and Teresa Burnham. Their love and support made this book and so much more possible.

---

1. http://github.com/jashkenas/coffee-script/contributors

Introduction

JavaScript was never meant to be the most important programming language in the world. It was hacked together in ten days, with ideas from Scheme and Self packed into a C-like syntax. Even its name was an awkward fit, referring to a language with little in common besides a few keywords. (For the story behind that, see Peter Seibel's interview with Brendan Eich, the creator of JavaScript, in *Coders at Work [Sei09]*.) But once JavaScript was released, there was no controlling it. As the only language understood by all major browsers, JavaScript quickly became the lingua franca of the Web. And with the introduction of Ajax in the early 2000s, what began as a humble scripting language for enhancing web pages suddenly became a full-fledged rich application development language.

As JavaScript's star rose, discontent came from all corners. Some pointed to its numerous little quirks and inconsistencies.[1] Others complained about its lack of classes and inheritance. And a new generation of coders, who had cut their teeth on Ruby and Python, were stymied by its thickets of curly braces, parentheses, and semicolons.

A brave few created frameworks for web application development that generated JavaScript code from other languages, notably Google's GWT and 280 North's Objective-J. But few programmers wanted to add a thick layer of abstraction between themselves and the browser. No, they would press on, dealing with JavaScript's flaws by limiting themselves to "the good parts" (as in the title of Douglas Crockford's now-classic book).

And then CoffeeScript came along.

The New Kid in Town

On Christmas Day 2009, Jeremy Ashkenas first released CoffeeScript, a little language he touted as "JavaScript's less ostentatious kid brother." The project

---

1.   http://wtfjs.com/

quickly attracted hundreds of followers on GitHub as Ashkenas and other contributors added a bevy of improvements each month. The language's compiler, originally written in Ruby, was replaced in March 2010 by one written in CoffeeScript.

After its 1.0 release on Christmas 2010, CoffeeScript became one of GitHub's "most watched" projects. And the language attracted another flurry of attention in April 2011, when David Heinemeier Hansson confirmed rumors that CoffeeScript support would be included in Ruby on Rails 3.1.

Why did this little language catch on so quickly? Three reasons come to mind: familiarity, safety, and readability.

The Good Parts Are Still There

JavaScript is a vast language. It contains multitudes of features, which obscure its essence. JavaScript offers many of the benefits of a functional language while retaining the familiar feel of an imperative one. This subtle power is one of the reasons that JavaScript tends to confound newcomers. Functions can be passed around as arguments and returned from other functions, and objects can have new methods added at any time. In short, *functions are first-class objects*.

All that power is still there in CoffeeScript, but with a syntax that encourages you to use it wisely. Gone is the function keyword, along with its accompanying curly braces. Instead, blocks of function code are demarcated with -> or => and indentation. Likewise, the crucial yet often baffling this keyword has a distinctive symbol to serve in its stead, @. These are small changes, but they go a long way toward making the way a program works more obvious.

The Compiler Is Here to Help

Imagine a language with no syntax errors, a language where the computer forgives you your typos and tries as best it can to comprehend the code you give it. What a wonderful world that would be! Sure, the program wouldn't always run the way you expected, but hey, that's what testing is for.

Now imagine that you write that code once and send it out to the world, typos and all, and millions of computers work around your small mistakes in subtly different ways. Suddenly statements that your computer silently skipped over are crashing your entire app for thousands of users.

Sadly, that's the world we live in. JavaScript has no standard interpreter. Instead, hundreds of browsers and other environments run JavaScript in their own way. Debugging cross-platform inconsistencies is a huge pain.

CoffeeScript can't cure all of these ills, but the compiler tries its best to generate JavaScript Lint-compliant output,[2] which is a great filter for common human errors and nonstandard idioms. And if you type something that just doesn't make any sense, such as 2 = 3, the CoffeeScript compiler will tell you. Better to find out sooner than later.

It's All So Clear Now

Writing CoffeeScript can be highly addictive. Why? Take this piece of Java-Script:

```javascript
function cube(num) {
  return Math.pow(num, 3);
}
var list = [1, 2, 3, 4, 5];
var cubedList = [];
for (var i = 0; i < list.length; i++) {
  cubedList.push(cube(list[i]));
}
```

Now here's an equivalent snippet of CoffeeScript:

```coffeescript
cube = (num) -> Math.pow num, 3
list = [1, 2, 3, 4, 5]
cubedList = (cube num for num in list)
```

For those of you keeping score, that's half the character count and less than half the line count! Those kinds of gains are common in CoffeeScript. And as Paul Graham once put it, "Succinctness is power."[3]

Shorter code is easier to read, easier to write, and, perhaps most critically, easier to change. Gigantic heaps of code tend to lumber along, as any significant modifications require a Herculean effort. But bite-sized pieces of code can be revamped in a few swift keystrokes, encouraging a more agile, iterative development style.

It's worth adding that switching to CoffeeScript isn't an all-or-nothing proposition—CoffeeScript code and JavaScript code can interact freely. CoffeeScript's strings are just JavaScript strings, and its numbers are just JavaScript numbers. Even its classes work in JavaScript frameworks like Backbone.js.[4] So don't be afraid of calling JavaScript code from CoffeeScript code or vice versa. We'll talk about using CoffeeScript with two of JavaScript's

---

2.   http://www.javascriptlint.com/
3.   http://www.paulgraham.com/power.html
4.   http://documentcloud.github.com/backbone/

most popular libraries in Chapter 5, *Web Applications with jQuery and Backbone.js*, on page 49.

But enough ancient history. Coding is believing, everything else is just meta, and as Jeff Atwood once said, "Meta is murder."[5] So let's talk a little bit about the book you're reading now, and then—in just a few pages, I promise!—we'll start banging out some code.

Who This Book Is For

If you're interested in learning CoffeeScript, you've come to the right place! However, because CoffeeScript is so closely linked to JavaScript, there are really two languages running through this book—and not enough pages to teach you both. Therefore, I'm going to assume that you know *some* JavaScript.

You don't have to be John "JavaScript Ninja" Resig. In fact, if you're only an amateur JavaScripter, great! You'll learn a lot about JavaScript as you go through this book. Check the footnotes for links to additional resources that I recommend. If you're new to programming entirely, you should definitely check out *Eloquent JavaScript [Hav11]*, which is also available in an interactive online format.[6] If you've dabbled a bit but want to become an expert, pick up *Effective JavaScript [Her12]*.[7] And if you want a comprehensive reference, no one does it better than the Mozilla Developer Network.[8]

You may notice that I talk about Ruby a lot in this book. Ruby inspired many of CoffeeScript's great features, such as implicit returns, splats, and postfix conditionals. And thanks to the Rails Asset Pipeline, which makes CoffeeScript compilation fully automatic, CoffeeScript has a huge following in the Ruby world. So if you're a Rubyist, *great!* You've got a head start. If not, don't sweat it; everything will fall into place once you have a few examples under your belt.

If anything in the book doesn't make sense to you, I encourage you to post a question about it on the book's forum.[9] While I try to be clear, the only entities to whom programming languages are completely straightforward are computers —and they buy very few books.

---

5. http://www.codinghorror.com/blog/2009/07/meta-is-murder.html
6. http://eloquentjavascript.net/
7. http://effectivejs.com/
8. https://developer.mozilla.org/en/JavaScript/Guide
9. https://forums.pragprog.com/forums/347

Embedding JavaScript in CoffeeScript

This is as good a place as any to mention that you can stick JavaScript inside of CoffeeScript code by surrounding it with backticks, like so:

```
console.log `impatient ? useBacktivks() : learnCoffeeScript()`
```

The CoffeeScript compiler simply ignores everything between the backticks. That means that if, for instance, you declare a variable between the backticks, that variable won't obey conventional CoffeeScript scope rules.

In all my time writing CoffeeScript, I've never once needed to use backtick escapes. They're an eyesore at best and dangerous at worst. So in the immortal words of Troy McClure: "Now that you know how it's done—don't do it."

How This Book Is Organized

We'll start our journey by introducing the tools you'll need to compile, run, and debug CoffeeScript code. After that, the next three chapters will take you through the nuts and bolts of the language. Each of those chapters includes a small command-line project at the end. Finally, the last three chapters are dedicated to building and testing a Trello-like web application called Coffee-Tasks.

To master CoffeeScript, you'll need to know how it works with the rest of the JavaScript universe. So after learning the basics of the language, we'll take brief tours of jQuery, the world's most popular JavaScript framework, and Node.js, an exciting new project that lets you run JavaScript outside of the browser. While we won't go into great depth with either tool, we'll see that they go with CoffeeScript like chocolate and peanut butter. And by combining their powers, we'll be able to write an entire task management app in a matter of hours.

The code presented in this book, as well as errata and discussion forums, can be found on its PragProg page: http://pragprog.com/titles/tbcoffee2/coffeescript

What's Changed Since CoffeeScript 1.0.0?

Despite being a very young language, CoffeeScript has been remarkably stable in the years since its 1.0.0 release. As of this writing, the latest release is 1.8.0. For the most part, code written for CoffeeScript 1.0.0 will be accepted by the CoffeeScript 1.8.0 compiler, and vice versa. The few exceptions mainly have to do with syntactic edge cases involving implicit parentheses and indentation. Those who like to keep their code as paren-free as possible will be happy to know that ever since CoffeeScript 1.7.0, chaining code like this has worked as expected:

```
$('h1')
  .slideDown 100, => $('h2').show()
  .fadeIn 300
```

Personally, I prefer to use explicit parentheses in most cases, and you'll see that preference expressed in the code shown throughout this book. But this change has definitely made CoffeeScript's behavior in the absence of parentheses more aligned with human expectations.

But perhaps the biggest leap CoffeeScript has taken in the last few years is not in the language itself, but in the tooling. Since CoffeeScript 1.6.1, the compiler has included the ability to generate source maps, a debugger's dream come true. Before that, having to look at compiled JavaScript when an error was thrown was one of the most frequent complaints developers had about CoffeeScript. Happily, source maps solve that problem. We'll talk more about source maps in *Using Source Maps*, on page 5.

Another tooling addition is Literate CoffeeScript, which embodies an approach to coding advocated by the great Donald Knuth. In a .coffee file, you embed comments in code. But in a .litcoffee file, you do the opposite, writing a document in Markdown syntax with embedded snippets of code. The compiler simply extracts those snippets and ignores the rest of the code. The result is a human-readable narrative that doubles as a machine-readable program. Although I don't use Literate CoffeeScript in this book, I definitely think it's a cool concept.

For a (nearly) comprehensive list of changes the CoffeeScript project has gone through over time, see the changelog.[10]

The CoffeeScript Community

A great language is of little use without a strong community. If you run into problems, who you gonna call?

Posting a question to StackOverflow[11] (being sure to give your question the coffeescript tag) is a terrific way to get help, especially if you include a snippet of the code that's hassling you. If you need a more immediate answer, you can usually find friendly folks in the #coffeescript channel on Freenode IRC. For more problems, such as possible bugs, you should create an issue on

---

10. http://coffeescript.org/#changelog
11. http://stackoverflow.com

GitHub.[12] You can also request new language features there. CoffeeScript is still evolving, and the whole team welcomes feedback.

What about documentation? You've probably already seen the snazzy official docs.[13] There's also an official wiki.[14] And now there's this book.

Which brings us to me. I run @CoffeeScript on Twitter; you can reach me there or by good old-fashioned email at trevorburnham@gmail.com.

These are exciting times for web development. Welcome aboard!

---

12. http://github.com/jashkenas/coffee-script/issues
13. http://coffeescript.org
14. http://github.com/jashkenas/coffee-script/wiki

## CHAPTER 1

Getting Started

Before we get into the nitty-gritty of CoffeeScript syntax, let's make sure our yaks are properly shaved. In this chapter, we'll install the CoffeeScript compiler and get your editor of choice set up. After that, you'll be ready to dive in and code for the rest of this book.

You'll also see how CoffeeScript fits in with your development environment, whether you're coding for Rails, Node, or just a simple web page. With the right tools, using CoffeeScript should be just as easy as using JavaScript.

Installing CoffeeScript

The CoffeeScript compiler is written in CoffeeScript. That presents a chicken-and-egg problem: how do we run the compiler on a system that doesn't already have the CoffeeScript compiler? If only there were some way to run JavaScript on your machine without a web browser and give that code access to the local file system....

Ah, but there is: Node.js! If you haven't used Node before, don't worry about it; you'll learn more about it in Chapter 6, *Web Servers with Node and Express*, on page 69. For now, all you need to know is that Node is a bridge between JavaScript code and your operating system.

The rest of this section will be about installing Node and npm, which we need in order to use CoffeeScript's official coffee compiler. But if you're in a rush to get your feet wet, you might want to head over to the CoffeeScript site,[1] hit the Try CoffeeScript button, open your browser's development console, and skip ahead to the next chapter.

---

1. http://coffeescript.org/

Installing Node.js

Let's check whether you already have a reasonably up-to-date version of Node installed. Run this command:

```
$ node -v
v0.10.24
```

For this book, you'll want to have Node 0.10.x. If you're already there, feel free to skip to the next section.

Note that releases with odd minor version numbers, such as 0.9.x or 0.11.x, are considered "unstable," with experimental features and fluctuating APIs. If you're running one of those, consider switching to a stable release.

Installing the latest stable Node release on your system is very easy: just go to the Node.jps site,[2] download a binary installer, and run it.

If you feel like you might need multiple Node versions on your system (say, because Node 0.10 is obsolete by the time you're reading this), check out nvm.[3] (If you're a Windows user, try nvmw.)[4] It's the Node world's equivalent to rvm, the Ruby Version Manager. Once you have nvm installed, you can easily install and switch between specific node versions:

```
$ nvm install 0.10
$ nvm use 0.10
$ node -v
v0.10.24
```

Note that nvm's version-switching works by modifying your shell's PATH. As a result, your selected version of Node won't be exposed to other processes (such as your text editor) unless you create a symlink yourself.

However you installed Node, you should now find yourself with two new commands on your PATH: node and npm. npm is Node's package manager, the equivalent of Ruby's gem. I like npm a lot. In fact, I like it so much that I wrote a short book on it.[5]

You'll need npm for the next section, so check that you have it:

```
$ npm -v
1.3.21
```

---

2. http://nodejs.org
3. https://github.com/creationix/nvm
4. https://github.com/hakobera/nvmw
5. https://leanpub.com/npm

If you somehow wound up with Node and not npm, you should try a different Node installation method. Once you're set up with both, we can start Coffee-Scripting.

Installing the coffee-script Package

Run this command:

```
$ npm install -g coffee-script@1.8.0
/usr/local/bin/coffee -> /usr/local/lib/node_modules/coffee-script/bin/coffee
/usr/local/bin/cake -> /usr/local/lib/node_modules/coffee-script/bin/cake
coffee-script@1.8.0 /usr/local/lib/node_modules/coffee-script
```

This command tells npm: "Globally install version 1.8.0 of the coffee-script package." The -g ("global") option tells npm that we want this package to be visible throughout the system, not just in the current directory. Thanks to this option, npm tells us that it has taken that package's two command-line utilities (coffee and cake) and placed symlinks to them in /usr/local/bin.

cake is CoffeeScript's equivalent of make or rake. It's primarily intended as an internal tool for developing the CoffeeScript compiler, so we won't use it in this book. What we really want from the coffee-script package is coffee. Check that it installed properly:

```
$ coffee -v
CoffeeScript version 1.8.0
```

If you get "command not found," npm's target directory for binaries isn't on your PATH. You could change PATH, or you could change npm's target directory. For example:

```
$ npm config set prefix "/usr"
$ sudo npm install -g coffee-script@1.8.0
/usr/bin/coffee -> /usr/local/lib/node_modules/coffee-script/bin/coffee
/usr/bin/cake -> /usr/local/lib/node_modules/coffee-script/bin/cake
coffee-script@1.8.0 /usr/local/lib/node_modules/coffee-script
```

Note that we need sudo here because, unlike /usr/local, /usr is owned by the root user. Having to use sudo with npm is less than ideal, so I recommend finding or creating a directory you can own (say, ~/npm), adding it to your PATH, and setting it as npm's prefix. For more information on how to control where npm installs files, see the npm documentation.[6]

Now that you can run coffee, we can finally get to the fun part: writing code!

---

6. https://www.npmjs.org/doc/files/npm-folders.html

Running and Compiling CoffeeScript

Like most scripting languages, CoffeeScript has a REPL ("read-eval-print loop," a term that originated with Lisp) where you can run commands interactively. To enter the REPL, just run coffee:

```
$ coffee
coffee> audience = 'world'
'world'
coffee> "Hello, #{audience}!"
'Hello, world!'
```

To exit the REPL, press Ctrl-d.

The REPL handily shows you the output of each expression you enter. However, editing nontrivial amounts of code on the REPL is a pain. So how do we make coffee evaluate code written in our favorite text editor?

Create a file named hello.coffee with this code:

GettingStarted/hello.coffee
```
rl = require('readline').createInterface
  input: process.stdin
  output: process.stdout

rl.question "To whom am I speaking? ", (audience) ->
  console.log("Hello, #{audience}!")
```

Save the file and run it with coffee hello.coffee:

```
$ To whom am I speaking? Trevor
Hello, Trevor!
```

Behind the scenes, this command compiles hello.coffee into JavaScript and runs the resulting code. Let's try performing those steps separately so that we can look at the JavaScript output. Run the same command, but with the -c ("compile") flag. You should now have a file named hello.js in the same directory. Try running it with node hello.js. (Notice how coffee imitates node's command syntax whenever possible.)

The coffee command has many more tricks up its sleeve, but we won't be using them in this book. Instead, we'll use Grunt[7] in later chapters to do the heavy lifting of turning CoffeeScript source into production-ready JavaScript.

---

7. http://gruntjs.com/

Using Source Maps

When CoffeeScript was first released in 2009, source maps were but a twinkle in some Google engineers' eyes. The problem of debugging obfuscated Java-Script has existed ever since the dawn of web development, thanks to minification. Google decided to try to tackle the problem in their minification tool, Closure Compiler, by creating metadata called *source maps* that their Closure Inspector tool could parse. This metadata allowed pieces of minified code to be mapped to the original source code during debugging. In 2011, Google moved to add source maps to the debugging tools in WebKit, the engine underlying Safari and Chrome. (Google would later fork WebKit into a new engine called Blink.) Mozilla and Microsoft followed their lead. Today, all major browsers support the source map spec.

With source maps, compiled JavaScript can be delivered to the browser just as it would be otherwise: compiled, concatenated, and minified for maximum efficiency. The only overhead is a single comment (called the "pragma") containing the path (relative or absolute) of the script's corresponding source map, which conventionally has the same name as the script with the addition of the file extension .map:

```
//# sourceMappingURL=myScript.js.map
```

The comment is ignored when an ordinary user visits the page. But if you pop open the developer tools, the browser will try to load that map file. The map file, in turn, will tell the browser where it can find the original source file (or files) that were compiled into the script. Once the browser has downloaded all of those files, the developer tools will be able to provide much richer debugging information.

In the context of CoffeeScript, source maps mean that the longstanding dream of debugging CoffeeScript code in the browser—seeing the line of CoffeeScript code from which an error was thrown rather than seeing only the compiled JavaScript—can finally be realized. The development language and the production language are finally one and the same, provided that you've set up a build and deployment pipeline that generates the proper source maps and makes them available to the browser.

In later chapters, we'll use Grunt to generate source maps alongside our compiled JavaScript and ensure that those files end up where they need to be. We'll also see how source map debugging can be added to Node.js for server-side applications written in CoffeeScript. If you want to give source maps a whirl right now, just run the compiler with the -m (shorthand for --map) flag:

```
$ coffee -c -m myScript.coffee
$ ls -1
myScript.coffee
myScript.js
myScript.map
```

A note for Rails users: as of this writing, Sprockets (the Rails asset pipeline) does not support source maps. But don't be discouraged! Source map support is a top priority for the next major release, Sprockets 4.0.[8] I'm excited about this because it should make source maps "just work" in Rails, all the way from development to production. In the meantime, a plugin is available to generate CoffeeScript source maps in development mode.[9]

Editing CoffeeScript

For the next few chapters, you'll be learning the CoffeeScript language by running short examples. To get the most out of this experience, I highly recommend entering these examples into your favorite editor, taking advantage of the best available CoffeeScript plugins for syntax highlighting and execution without switching to the shell.

Personally, I use Sublime Text 3, a sleek, modern editor that runs natively across all major platforms. Maybe you prefer a more old-school editor, such as Vim or Emacs. Or maybe you're into rich IDEs, such as Eclipse or IntelliJ. No matter what editor you use, there's a good chance that someone has written CoffeeScript integration for it. A good first place to look is a page on the CoffeeScript wiki.[10]

Most plugins rely on the coffee utility you installed earlier in this chapter to compile and run CoffeeScript, so you may need to tell the plugin where that utility (and perhaps also node) can be found. You can track down those paths with which (or its Windows equivalent, where):

```
$ which coffee
/usr/local/bin/coffee
```

Before proceeding to the next chapter, make sure you have a plugin that gives you the ability to run the CoffeeScript file you're editing (and show you the output) with a single keystroke. Trust me: you'll have a lot more fun that way.

---

8. https://github.com/sstephenson/sprockets
9. https://github.com/markbates/coffee-rails-source-maps
10. https://github.com/jashkenas/coffee-script/wiki/Text-editor-plugins

## CHAPTER 2

Functions, Scope, and Context

The heart and soul of CoffeeScript consists of two characters: ->. That's all it takes to define a new function, but don't let the terseness fool you; as you'll soon see, functions are powerful, versatile objects. Mastering them is the first step to mastering CoffeeScript.

While functions are the major players of this chapter, you'll meet a cheerful supporting cast along the way: variables, strings, conditionals, and everything else you need to write useful functions. You'll also get a refresher on two crucial concepts, scope and context, and see how they map to CoffeeScript.

If you're an experienced JavaScripter, much of this chapter will be review. But keep an eye out for some of CoffeeScript's most useful features: property arguments, default arguments, and splats.

Functions 101

Fire up your favorite text editor and create a new .coffee file, because it's time to call our first function:

```
console.log 'Hello, functions!'
```

Hit your editor's Run command, and you'll get this greeting:

```
Hello, functions!
```

No surprises there. The only CoffeeScript-specific feature we're taking advantage of is *implicit parentheses*, which allows us to pass arguments to console.log without wrapping them in ().

Now let's make things a little more interesting:

```
console.log (-> 'Hello, IIFE!')()
```

```
Hello, IIFE!
```

What happened? Let's break it down:

1. `->` defines a function. CoffeeScript uses these two characters in lieu of JavaScript's `function` keyword.

2. The function returns the string `'Hello, IIFE!'` because CoffeeScript functions have *implicit returns* (one of many features borrowed from Ruby).

3. Putting `()` after the function expression causes it to be called, and the result of that call is passed to `console.log`.

The pattern of defining a function and calling it right away is so ubiquitous in JavaScript and CoffeeScript that it has its own name: *IIFE* (pronounced "iffy"), an Immediately Invoked Function Expression.

Functions are first-class objects in JavaScript, meaning that they can be passed around and assigned to variables just like any other type:

```
returnGreeting = -> 'Hello, function variable!'
console.log returnGreeting()

Hello, function variable!
```

A technical point that bears mentioning: CoffeeScript does not support *named functions*, a JavaScript feature that allows functions to be called before they're defined. The main reason for this is a thorny issue in older versions of IE. For details, see the CoffeeScript FAQ.[1]

Taking Arguments

So far, all of the functions we've defined have simply returned constants. Unfortunately, practical code requires a bit more variety. Let's define a function with an *argument list*:

```
greet = (subject) -> "Hello, #{subject}!"
console.log greet 'argument'

Hello, argument!
```

This syntax may take some getting used to. Whereas JavaScript and other C-inspired languages put the argument list at the end of the function declaration (`function(arg1, arg2)`, CoffeeScript puts it first (`(arg1, arg2) ->`).

The other CoffeeScript syntax on display here is *string interpolation*. CoffeeScript's interpolation syntax is similar to Ruby's: `"A#{expression}Z"` is equivalent to `'A' + (expression) + 'Z'`.

1.　https://github.com/jashkenas/coffee-script/wiki/FAQ

Multiline Functions

Because we don't live in a perfect world, not all functions you'll want to write are one-liners. Here we reach one of the most controversial aspects of Coffee-Script: it's a *whitespace-sensitive language*. To define a CoffeeScript function with more than one line, you indent the function body:

```
getCurrentDate = ->
  now = new Date
  "#{now.getMonth()}/#{now.getDay()}, #{now.getFullYear()}"
```

Note that I've used two spaces for indentation, as I will throughout this book. The CoffeeScript compiler doesn't impose a standard unit of indentation, but it's important to be consistent within each file you edit. Also, be sure to avoid mixing tabs and spaces! If you want an automated tool to help keep your team's code style consistent, check out CoffeeLint.[2]

The same whitespace rule applies to all other language constructs in the CoffeeScript language. Here's a function with a conditional:

```
pluralize = (count, word, suffix = 's') ->
  if count is 1
    word
  else
    word + suffix
```

We'll explain the suffix = 's' in the next section. As an aside, notice that this function works without an explicit return. One of CoffeeScript's core tenets is, "Everything is an expression." An *expression* is a statement that has a value. In JavaScript, conditionals have no value (unless written with the ternary operator). In CoffeeScript, they do.

You can write conditionals on one line using the then keyword to separate the condition from the body.

```
  if strikes >= 3 then out()
</Code>

<p>
  CoffeeScript also allows <firstuse>postfix
  conditionals</firstuse>, such as
</p>

<code language="coffeescript">
  out() if strikes >= 3
```

---

2.   http://www.coffeelint.org/

As a personal preference, I tend toward multiline conditionals, for a practical reason: I like having the ability to change a condition and its body as two separate, nonconflicting Git commits.

The Existential Operator and Default Arguments

Some languages, such as C++, allow different functions with the same name to be defined to take different numbers of arguments. That's not the case in JavaScript, which is a dynamic language that allows any function to take any number of arguments. (As you'll see in the next section, even arguments beyond those named in the function's argument list can be used.) Instead, we need to put conditional logic inside the function to make it behave differently depending on whether an argument has been passed.

To check that a variable has a value (more precisely, that it's neither null nor undefined), we can use the *existential operator*, expressed as a question mark:

```
if i?
  think()
```

The existential operator can also be used between two values to mean "the first variable if it has a value, the second variable if it doesn't":

```
myChoice = firstChoice ? secondChoice
```

Finally, the existential operator has an assignment form, which means "if this variable doesn't already have a value, assign this value":

```
dinner ?= 'macAndCheese'
```

On a per-character basis, I'd say the existential operator is the most powerful feature in CoffeeScript. But for the use case of assigning default values to omitted function arguments, there's an even terser syntax:

```
buyAnything = (retailer = 'amazon') ->
```

This *default argument* syntax is equivalent to writing retailer ?= 'amazon' at the top of the function body. If the function is called with no arguments, the value of retailer will be undefined, so the default value will be assigned.

Splatted Arguments

Let's say you want to take a long list of arguments and turn all or part of it into an array. As any veteran JavaScripter could tell you, every function has an array-like object arguments with methods for accessing all of the arguments that were passed in for that function call. That object can be turned into a proper array through careful application of the slice method. CoffeeScript makes things a bit easier:

```
showOff = (allArguments...) ->
  console.log allArguments
```

The trailing ellipsis means that allArguments "soaks" all of the arguments from that position forward. allArguments will always be an array:

```
showOff()
showOff('once', 'twice', 'thrice')

[]
['once', 'twice', 'thrice']
```

You can use splats on the calling side of a function call as well. Whereas splatted arguments transform a list of arguments into an array, splatted function calls transform an array into a list of arguments. An excellent use case for this is passing an array to Math.min:

```
numbers = [5.4, 9.4, 1.8, 2.2]
console.log Math.min(numbers...)

1.8
```

As you'll see in the next chapter, splats are also useful for constructing and extracting values from arrays.

Variable Scope

You need to know three rules to understand scoping in CoffeeScript:

1. Every function creates its own scope.

2. Functions are the *only* constructs that create scope.

3. Each variable lives in the outermost scope in which a value is (potentially) assigned to it.

The first two rules are an innate part of the JavaScript language. (More precisely, it's how variables are scoped with the var keyword. A different scoping keyword, let, is also supported in the ECMAScript 6 draft spec and a handful of forward-looking JavaScript runtimes.) CoffeeScript follows suit, which means that conditionals and loops do not create scope.

The last rule allows CoffeeScript to do away with var. If you write myBologna = 'Oscar Mayer', it's understood that you want to create a local variable named myBologna. JavaScript, by contrast, would give that variable global scope unless explicitly told to do otherwise. Be warned, however, that this rule can exacer-

bate the problem of *shadowing*, where what was intended as a variable declaration instead overwrites the value of an existing variable. Take care not to
use the same variable name in two different, nested scopes.

All Functions Are Closures

One of JavaScript's distinctive features is that all functions are *closures*,
meaning that they have access to all variables in all surrounding scopes—
regardless of where they're called from. CoffeeScript inherits this important
semantic. To give a trivial example:

```
X = 5
sumXY = -> X + Y
Y = 7
console.log sumXY()
```

```
12
```

Both X and Y are declared in the scope surrounding sumXY, so the function
has access to both variables. It doesn't matter that Y isn't mentioned until
after the function declaration. Variable scope is determined at compile time.
Assigning a value to Y anywhere in that scope is sufficient to make Y live there.

Now let's look at a trickier example:

```
showCount = (->
  count = 0
  ->
    count += 1
    console.log count
)()
showCount()
showCount()
showCount()
```

```
1
2
3
```

Let's break this down:

1. The inner function is defined to increment count and then display that
   value.

2. The IIFE declares count, assigns it an initial value of 0, and returns the
   inner function.

3. Because the inner function is returned by the IIFE, that's what gets
   assigned to showCount.

So in the outermost scope, the count variable is hidden from us. But it's accessible to showCount because that function is defined within the scope where count lives.

Other languages have features such as "private variables" and "static variables." JavaScript and CoffeeScript don't. Instead, functions give you as much control over variable scope as you want.

Capturing Variables

Although closures are a powerful tool, they do lead to counterintuitive behavior. Here's an example adapted from another book I wrote:

```
for i in [1, 2, 3]
  setTimeout (-> console.log i), 0

3
3
3
```

The loop iterates over the numbers 1, 2, and 3, so why is the output the number 3 three times? Because when the function is defined and when it's passed to setTimeout are irrelevant. All that matters is the value of i when the function runs. And setTimeout won't run the function passed to it until after the loop has finished, even if the timeout is 0.

How can we fix this? What we need to do is take the value at the time of the loop iteration and *capture* it somehow. We could use an array or a hash to store this information, but an easier and more general solution is to define a function on each loop iteration with our value as an argument. For example:

```
for i in [1, 2, 3]
  do (i) ->
    setTimeout (-> console.log i), 0

1
2
3
```

do is a CoffeeScript keyword designed expressly for this purpose: it calls the given function, passing in the variables whose names match those of the arguments. (Remember how I warned you about variable shadowing? This is the one form of shadowing I approve of, since the relationship between the outer i and the inner i is clear.)

I should mention that creating functions on each loop iteration is a bit wasteful. In the three lines above, we've managed to allocate six functions— two for each loop iteration. In a loop with several orders of magnitude more repetitions, this would have a real performance impact. Then again, so would setting that many timeouts!

Execution Context

JavaScript has two special objects that are created every time a function is called: this and arguments. I mentioned arguments once before, in *Splatted Arguments*, on page 10, and I won't mention it again. But this is part of JavaScript's core essence. It allows functions to be used as *methods*, meaning that they can be attached to an object and know which object they're attached to. Here's a simple example:

```
fry = {}
fry.name = 'Philip J. Fry'
fry.sayName = -> console.log(this.name)
fry.sayName()
```

```
Philip J. Fry
```

The magic here is that JavaScript and CoffeeScript read the statement fry.sayName() to mean "call the function fry.sayName in the context of fry." The fact that we assigned the function to fry.sayName as soon as we defined it is irrelevant. We could have defined the function on its own first and then attached it to fry later, and we'd still get the same result. In Chapter 4, *Classes, Prototypes, and Inheritance*, on page 35, we'll see how this and special objects called prototypes make classic object-oriented programming possible in JavaScript.

Because this is so important, CoffeeScript allows the @ symbol to be used as a synonym for it. My preference is to always use @, since it stands out so clearly in code, and treating this like an ordinary variable is a recipe for disaster. I'll use @ instead of this (and @x instead of this.x) in the code examples for the remainder of the book.

Controlling Context

When you call a function by writing obj.func(), func is called in the context of obj. If you call a function directly by writing func(), then func is called in the context of the *root object*. In the browser, this root object is window. In Node, it's called global.

But let's say you want to control the context of a function call. You can do that using two methods that are attached to every function: call and apply. Both take the context (that is, the object that will become this in the function call) as their first argument. call passes all subsequent arguments along to the function:

```
tribble = {count: 2}
multiply = (multiplier) -> @count *= multiplier
multiply.call(tribble, 16)
console.log tribble.count
```

32

Meanwhile, apply takes an array as its second argument and expands that into a list of arguments for the function. If this reminds you of the splatted calls we learned about earlier, that's not a coincidence! apply is how splatted calls are implemented. So these two expressions are precisely equivalent:

```
console.log Math.min.apply(Math, numbers)
```

```
console.log Math.min(numbers...)
```

Keep in mind that you can always use splats instead of apply, *as long as the context you want is the same as the object to which the function is attached.*

Bound Functions

The mercurial nature of this, changing on every function call, is one of the most common causes of JavaScript confusion. While this is supremely useful, there are times when we want a function we define to only use the value of this in the surrounding function. This is especially common for *callbacks*, functions passed as arguments to other functions.

Luckily, CoffeeScript gives us a dedicated syntax for *bound functions*, whose this value is fixed to be the same as it is where they're defined. All we need to do is write => instead of ->:

```
majorTom = {secondsLeft: 4}
majorTom.countDown = ->
  setTimeout (=>
    console.log @secondsLeft
    @secondsLeft--
    if @secondsLeft > 0
      @countDown()
  ), 1000
majorTom.countDown()
```

4
3
2
1

If we'd written the timeout function with ->, it would be called in the root object context, so @secondsLeft and @countDown would be undefined.

Internally, the CoffeeScript compiler uses an old trick to accomplish this feat, copying the outer function's this to a variable and replacing bound functions' references to this with references to that variable. Condensing that technique down to a one-character change is the essence of what CoffeeScript does for developers. And because the this copy is made only when needed, you can use => freely with no impact on performance—except when defining class methods, as you'll see in *Classes: Giving Prototypes Structure*, on page 38.

Mini-Project: Checkbook Balancer

Let's put these ideas together into an old-school computer program. All we want to do is keep track of where we're keeping our money across three accounts: checking, savings, and our mattress. We can deposit or withdraw money from each of these accounts. Let's implement these two actions as methods on an object that represents the account, and return that object from a function so that we can create as many accounts as we need without repeating our implementation code:

```
Functions/checkbooks/checkbooks.coffee
createAccount = (name) ->
  {
    name: name
    balance: 0

    description: ->
      "#{@name}: #{dollarsToString(@balance)}"

    deposit: (amount) ->
      @balance += amount
      @

    withdraw: (amount) ->
      @balance -= amount
      @
  }
```

(I hope you won't literally take this code to the bank. Remember to use ACID transactions when working with real money!)

Sharp-eyed readers will notice that I call a function here that I haven't defined yet: dollarsToString. That's okay; that function just has to be defined before description is called. We'll define it and one other utility function a bit later.

Notice that I've returned @ from each method, a common default for methods that have no obvious return value, since it allows calls to be chained: account.deposit(x).withdraw(y)

Let's create our three accounts:

Functions/checkbooks/checkbooks.coffee
```
checking = createAccount('Checking')
savings  = createAccount('Savings')
mattress = createAccount('Mattress')
```

In a perfect world, we'd just drop the code we've written into the CoffeeScript REPL, and everyone's financial problems would be solved. Instead, we're going to tack on a pretty user interface. And as is so often the case in software, the UI requires more work than the core of the application.

Node.js by itself makes it difficult to write interactive command-line programs. Fortunately, many libraries are perfectly suited to this purpose. We're going to use one called Inquirer.js,[3] which lets us build prompts with pizzazz. Let's go ahead and install it using npm. If you don't have a package.json, run through npm init first. Then:

```
$ npm install --save inquirer
```

The --save flag tells npm that in addition to downloading the package into our project's node_modules, it should also make a note of it in the project's package.json. That way, rather than checking node_modules into version control, we can just check in package.json. It's a solid Node practice to always keep your project's package.json in sync with node_modules.

Once a package is in node_modules, we can load it from our app code using Node's require function. For a detailed explanation of how require works, skip ahead to *Writing Node Modules*, on page 70.

We're going to use Inquirer to present the user with three prompts: one to choose the account, another to choose an action, and a third to choose an amount. Then we cycle back. Here's the code to do that:

Functions/checkbooks/checkbooks.coffee
```
inquirer = require('inquirer')

promptForAccount = ->
  inquirer.prompt({
    name: 'account'
    message: 'Pick an account:'
    type: 'list'
    choices: [
      {name: checking.description(), value: checking}
      {name: savings.description(), value: savings}
      {name: mattress.description(), value: mattress}
```

---

3. https://github.com/SBoudrias/Inquirer.js/

```
    ]
  }, (answers) ->
    account = answers.account
    promptForAction(account)
  )

promptForAction = (account) ->
  inquirer.prompt({
    name: 'action'
    message: 'Pick an action:'
    type: 'list'
    choices: [
      {name: 'Deposit $ into this account', value: 'deposit'}
      {name: 'Withdraw $ from this account', value: 'withdraw'}
    ]
  }, (answers) ->
    action = answers.action
    promptForAmount(account, action)
  )

promptForAmount = (account, action) ->
  inquirer.prompt({
    name: 'amount'
    message: "Enter the amount to #{action}:"
    type: 'input'
    validate: (input) =>
      if isNaN(inputToNumber(input))
        return 'Please enter a numerical amount.'
      if inputToNumber(input) < 0
        return 'Please enter a non-negative amount.'
      true
  }, (answers) ->
    amount = inputToNumber(answers.amount)
    account[action](amount)
    promptForAccount()
  )
```

Talking to humans is hard work! For each of the three prompts, we've given Inquirer some parameters telling it what to display and a callback that is invoked with the user's "answers." The answer to the last question asked is stored with a key corresponding to the name given for the prompt. That's why answers.account corresponds to the answer given for the account prompt, and so on.

I've snuck in one more as-yet-undefined utility function, inputToNumber. Before we define it, let's install the Numeral.js[4] currency formatting library, which our other mystery function (from createAccount) will need:

---

4. http://numeraljs.com/

```
$ npm install --save numeral
```

All of our dependencies are now in place, so we can define our utility functions:

Functions/checkbooks/checkbooks.coffee
```
numeral = require ('numeral')

dollarsToString = (dollars) ->
  numeral(dollars).format('$0,0.00')

inputToNumber = (input) ->
  parseFloat input.replace(/[$,]/g, ''), 10
```

Now all that's left to do is to fire the first prompt!

Functions/checkbooks/checkbooks.coffee
```
promptForAccount()
```

And with that, we're ready to run our first CoffeeScript program:

```
$ coffee checkbooks.coffee
[?] Pick an account: (Use arrow keys)
> Checking: $0.00
  Savings: $0.00
  Mattress: $0.00
```

Wow! Such Function! So Coffee!

It's safe to say that you now know more about CoffeeScript than 99.999 percent of the Earth's population. You've learned how to define, call, and return values from functions. More impressively, you've discovered what it means for a function to create scope and why the context variable this is such a fickle creature. You've also sampled a smorgasbord of CoffeeScript's other features—if/unless, try...catch, default argument values, and splats among them.

We haven't yet touched two big parts of CoffeeScript: collections (objects and arrays) and iteration (loops). By a happy coincidence, those are the subject of the next chapter.

## CHAPTER 3

Collections, Iteration, and Destructuring

All code is, at its core, about data: reading data, transforming data, and emitting data. As software developers, we're constantly tasked with designing the structures that contain this data. Luckily, JavaScript makes it easy to manipulate two of the most powerful structures known to computer science: arrays and hash maps. And CoffeeScript goes one step further, streamlining the syntax for working with these fundamental entities.

In this chapter, we'll start with a refresher on how the JavaScript language allows every object to serve a dual purpose as all-purpose storage. Then we'll get into arrays, which give us a more ordered place to save our bits. From there, we'll segue into loops, the lingua franca of iteration. We'll also learn about building arrays directly from loops and extracting parts of arrays and objects using destructuring.

Objects as Hash Maps

Every programming language worth its bits has some data structure that lets you store arbitrary named values. Whether you call them hash maps, dictionaries, or associative arrays, the core functionality is the same: you provide a key and a value, and then you use the key to fetch the value.

In JavaScript, every object is a hash map. And just about everything is an object: the only exceptions are the *primitives* (Booleans, numbers, and strings) and a few special constants, such as undefined and NaN. Because of the ubiquity of data-filled objects, CoffeeScript has several special features aimed at making it easier to work with them.

Creating Objects

A simple object is typically defined using the JSON-style syntax:

```
obj = {key: 'value'}
```

In JSON, objects are denoted by {}, arrays by []. Note that JSON is a subset of JavaScript for most practical purposes—though not strictly[1]—and can usually be pasted directly into CoffeeScript code. (The biggest exception is when the JSON contains indentation that might be misinterpreted by the CoffeeScript compiler.)

There are plenty of other ways to create objects. In fact, we created a ton of them in the previous chapter, because all functions are objects. (And functions, unlike other objects, can be used to create inheritance. More on that in the next chapter.) But most of the time, you'll want to use the JSON-style syntax.

CoffeeScript streamlines the JSON-style syntax by allowing you to omit the curly braces:

```
obj = key: 'value'
```

Additionally, you can omit the commas that normally separate key-value pairs, using line breaks as separators instead:

```
credentials =
  username: 'Yorick'
  password: 'h4m1371v3s'
```

Note that the keys are kept at the same level of indentation. This is important because the CoffeeScript compiler interprets indentation within an object definition as indicating a nested object:

```
sprite =
  image: 'blip.gif'
  position:
    x: 50
    y: 40
```

If you've worked with YAML, this syntax should look familiar.

Omitting curly braces is fun, but there's one case where they're very useful: when you want to define an object where a key is the same as the name of a variable. CoffeeScript allows you to eliminate this repetition:

```
position = if offScreen then 'absolute' else 'relative'
$el.css {position}  # equivalent to {position: position}
```

In the next section, we'll see that this syntax has an inverse as well.

---

1.   http://timelessrepo.com/json-isnt-a-javascript-subset

Using Objects

Once an object is defined, you're free to read its values and change it however you like. There are two equivalent syntaxes for reading and writing object values: dot notation (obj.x) and bracket notation (obj['x']). Usually you want to use dot notation if you know a key at compile time and bracket notation if you need to determine it at runtime. However, since keys can be arbitrary strings, you might sometimes need to use bracket notation with a literal key:

```
symbols.+ = 'plus'       # illegal syntax
symbols['+'] = 'plus'  # perfectly valid
```

One small nicety the CoffeeScript compiler provides is automatically replacing dot notation with bracket notation when you use a reserved keyword, because some JavaScript runtimes can't handle keywords being used that way. For example, symbols.if compiles to symbols["if"].

You can combine reading and writing from objects with the existential operator (previously described in *The Existential Operator and Default Arguments*, on page 10):

```
sprite?.coordinates  # read sprite.coordinates if sprite exists
sprite?.opacity = 1  # set sprite.opacity to 1 if sprite exists
```

You can chain the operator if you're uncertain about the existence of multiple nested objects:

```
console?.log?('Better safe than sorry!')
```

Another CoffeeScript feature allows you to read multiple values from an object into variables with a single expression. This is called *destructuring*:

```
{x, y} = coordinates
```

At first, this syntax looks backward. But like so much of CoffeeScript, there's an elegance to it. As you learned in the previous section, coordinates = {x, y} would define an object named coordinates and set its x and y values equal to the variables with the same name. The destructuring syntax is simply the inverse: rather than creating a new object, {x, y} = coordinates describes a pattern for reading object values into variables.

In practice, destructuring is most commonly seen in argument lists, where it allows a function to extract any number of values from a single object argument:

```
fire = ({x, y}) =>
  if x is 5 and y is 7
    console.log "You sunk my battleship!"
```

Be warned, however, that destructuring does not check for the existence of the object. Attempting to destructure an object that does not exist will result in an error.

Arrays

Let's say, hypothetically, that you have an ordered list of values. (A rarity in software, I know, but bear with me.) You could use any old object to store those values, but arrays (which inherit the properties of the Array prototype) offer you several nice conveniences.[2] They also, as a practical matter, improve performance by hinting that the JavaScript runtime should allocate a sequential block of memory.

Arrays can be defined using JSON-style syntax:

```
mcFlys = ['George', 'Lorraine', 'Marty']
```

All arrays in JavaScript are dynamic, with (practically) unlimited length. So you could define the exact same array one piece at a time:

```
mcFlys = []
mcFlys[0] = 'George'
mcFlys[1] = 'Lorraine'
mcFlys[2] = 'Marty'
```

The use of the same bracket notation that we had for objects is not coincidental. Arrays *are* objects! In fact, there's nothing special syntactically about using numbers to access array indices. Indices are just object keys, and all object keys are strings, so arr[1], arr['1'], and even arr[{toString: -> '1'}] (using an object with a toString method that controls how it's converted to a string) are synonymous. (When an object is used as a key, it's converted to the string returned by its toString method.) The only benefit we get from using numbers for array indices, aside from preserving our sanity, is having the length property set for us automatically when we insert a value with a higher index than had existed previously.

Now, all of the above is as true in JavaScript as it is in CoffeeScript, though it still sounds strange if you say it out loud. In the rest of this section, we'll see what CoffeeScript adds to the mix.

---

2.   http://developer.mozilla.org/en/JavaScript/Reference/Global_Objects/Array

Ranges

Fire up the REPL, because the best way to get acquainted with CoffeeScript range syntax—and its close friends, the slice and splice syntaxes, introduced in the next section—is ('practice' for i in [1..3]).join(', ').

CoffeeScript adds a Ruby-esque syntax for defining arrays of consecutive integers:

```
coffee> [1..5]
[1, 2, 3, 4, 5]
```

The .. defines an *inclusive range*. But often, we want to omit the last value; in those cases, we add an extra . to create an *exclusive range*:

```
coffee> [1...5]
[1, 2, 3, 4]
```

(As a mnemonic, picture the extra . replacing the end value.) Ranges can also go backward:

```
coffee> [5..1]
[5, 4, 3, 2, 1]
```

Regardless of the direction, an exclusive range omits the end value:

```
coffee> [5...1]
[5, 4, 3, 2]
```

This syntax is rarely used on its own, but as you'll soon see, it's essential to CoffeeScript's for loops.

Slicing and Splicing

When you want to tear a chunk out of a JavaScript array, you turn to the violent-sounding slice method:

```
coffee> ['a', 'b', 'c', 'd'].slice 0, 3
['a', 'b', 'c']
```

The two numbers given to slice are indices; everything from the first index up to *but not including* the second index is copied to the result. You might look at that and say, "That sounds like an exclusive range." And you'd be right:

```
coffee> ['a', 'b', 'c', 'd'][0...3]
['a', 'b', 'c']
```

And you can use an inclusive range, too:

```
coffee> ['a', 'b', 'c', 'd'][0..3]
['a', 'b', 'c', 'd']
```

The rules here are *slightly* different than they were for standalone ranges, though, due to the nature of slice. Notably, if the first index comes after the second, the result is an empty array rather than a reversal:

```
coffee> ['a', 'b', 'c', 'd'][3...0]
[]
```

Also, negative indices count backward from the end of the array. While arr[-1] merely looks for a property named '-1', arr[0...-1] means "Give me a slice from the start of the array up to, but not including, its last element." In other words, when slicing arr, -1 means the same thing as arr.length - 1:

```
coffee> ['a', 'b', 'c', 'd'][0...-1]
['a', 'b', 'c']
```

If you omit the second index, then the slice goes all the way to the end, whether you use two dots or three:

```
coffee> ['this', 'that', 'the other'][1..]
['that', 'the other']
coffee> ['this', 'that', 'the other'][1...]
['that', 'the other']
```

CoffeeScript also provides a shorthand for splice, the value-inserting cousin of slice. It looks like you're making an assignment to the slice:

```
coffee> arr = ['a', 'c']
coffee> arr[1...2] = ['b']
coffee> arr
['a', 'b']
```

The range defines the part of the array to be replaced. If the range is empty (like [1...1]), then there's an insertion at that point but no replacement:

```
coffee> arr = ['a', 'c']
coffee> arr[1...1] = ['b']
coffee> arr
['a', 'b', 'c']
coffee> arr[1..1] = ['2']
['a', 2, 'c']
```

One caveat: while negative indices work great for slicing, they fail completely when splicing. The trick of omitting the last index works fine, though:

```
coffee> steveAustin = ['regular', 'guy']
coffee> replacementParts = ['better', 'stronger', 'faster']
coffee> steveAustin[0..] = replacementParts
coffee> steveAustin
['better', 'stronger', 'faster']
```

Before we leave slices and splices behind, I should note that strings also happen to have a slice method. As a result, the same syntax that works for extracting a portion of an array can also be used to extract a substring:

```
coffee> 'The year is 3022'[-4..]
3022
```

Unfortunately, there is no native splice method for strings. Nor can you add one: JavaScript strings are immutable.

Iterating over Collections

I'll be honest: I don't like loops. Nine times out of ten, if I want to perform an operation on each item in a collection, I'm going to use one of the methods provided by a library like Underscore.js,[3] which allows the intent of the loop to be expressed more clearly than native syntax would allow.

Still, it's important as a programmer to understand the language capabilities available to you. These are, after all, the fundamental building blocks that libraries such as Underscore rely on, and there are situations where you'll want to put those building blocks together in novel ways. In this section, we'll see how CoffeeScript allows you to write powerful, succinct loops without invoking a utility function.

Loop Syntaxes

There are two built-in syntaxes for iterating over collections in CoffeeScript: one for iterating over object keys and another for iterating through arrays (and other types with numerical indices, but usually arrays). The two look similar, but they behave very differently.

To iterate over an object's properties, use the for...of syntax:

```
for key, value of object
  # do things with key and value
```

This loop will go through each of the object's keys. For each iteration, it assigns the key to the first variable named after the for. The second variable, if provided, is assigned the value corresponding to the key. So, value = object[key].

To iterate over an array, use for...in:

```
for value, index in array
  # do things with the value
```

---

3.   http://underscorejs.org/

Why use a separate syntax? Why not just use for key, value of array? Because there's nothing stopping an array from having extra values attached to non-numeric keys. Also, there's no order guaranteed when using for...of. So if you just want to treat the array as an array, use for...in. That way, you'll only get array[0], array[1], and so on up to array[array.length - 1].

As with for...of, the second variable in for...in is optional and is usually omitted. This is why the value comes first in array loops: you often don't need the index.

Conditional Iteration

Often, you'll want a loop to ignore some of a collection's entries. JavaScript allows you to do this by writing if (condition) continue at the top of the loop body. Because this is such a common technique, CoffeeScript provides a dedicated syntax for it:

```
for name, distance of stars when distance < 1e12
  planTravelToStar(name)
```

Note that the condition you provide to when is the negation of the condition you would use with if (condition) continue: the code above skips a loop iteration every time !(distance < 1e12).

Sometimes you'll want to iterate over all of an object's keys that are owned by that object, rather than being inherited from its prototype. (If you're unfamiliar with prototypes, you should look forward to the next chapter—specifically, *The Power of Prototypes*, on page 35.) You could do this with when object.hasOwnProperty(key). However, CoffeeScript allows you to use a single word instead:

```
for own sword of Kahless
  # ...
```

This is shorthand for the following:

```
for sword of Kahless
  continue unless Kahless.hasOwnProperty(sword)
  # ...
```

Accidentally iterating over prototype methods is an easy mistake to make. Whenever a for...of loop is giving you properties you didn't expect, try using for own...of instead.

Array Comprehensions

Recall from the previous chapter that one of CoffeeScript's core tenets is, "Everything is an expression." What, then, is a value of a loop expression? An array of the values of the loop's iterations, naturally. When a loop is used this way, it's called an *array comprehension*.

Array comprehensions are handy for transforming one array into another:

```
negativeNumbers = for num in [1, 2, 3, 4]
  -num
```

Of course, for a 1:1 mapping like this one, a map utility function would be just as succinct. But unlike map, array comprehensions can be combined with loop features like conditionals:

```
primeReciprocals = for num in [1, 2, 3, 4] when isPrime(num)
  1 / num
```

Array comprehensions can also be used with for's simpler cousins, while and until, allowing an unlimited number of iterations:

```
keysPressed = while(char = handleKeyPress())
  char
```

One word of warning: array comprehensions can be a performance hog when you're running a loop that you *don't* want to use to generate an array. The CoffeeScript compiler is smart enough to generate a comprehension only when you use the value of the loop, but thanks to implicit returns, it expects the value to be used any time you put a loop at the end of a function. The solution is to add an explicit return statement after the loop:

```
moveFlyingToasters = (toasters) ->
  for toaster in toasters
    toaster.x += 1
    toaster.y += 1
  return
```

As a matter of style, it's always good to put return at the end of your functions when you aren't returning a value.

Mini-Project: Refactored Checkbook Balancer

Let's take what we've learned from this chapter and use it to add a new feature to the checkbook balancer from *Mini-Project: Checkbook Balancer*, on page 16 —while making the code more maintainable!

The original checkbooks program allowed you to pick one of three accounts ("checking," "savings," and "mattress") and deposit or withdraw money from that account. The program had one limitation that made it slightly impractical: no persistence. When you closed the program, all account balances were reset to $0. The new checkbooks2 will remedy that by serializing account objects to a JSON file. We'll also add a "transfer" action that moves money from one account to another.

Let's start by creating a new directory for our project and installing the same dependencies as before:

```
$ npm init
$ npm install --save inquirer
$ npm install --save numeral
```

And we'll add one new one, jsonfile:[4]

```
$ npm install --save jsonfile
```

Now into the code! We're going to make three changes to our createAccount function. First, we're going to add a transfer method to the account object. Second, we're going to call a utility saveState function every time we perform an action. Third, we're going to switch from having argument lists to having a single "options" argument and extracting the values we want using the destructuring syntax. This gives us a lot more flexibility if we add new features to a function, because we don't have to add more and more arguments in an increasingly hard-to-remember order.

Collections/checkbooks2/checkbooks2.coffee
```coffee
createAccount = ({name}) ->
  {
    name: name
    balance: 0

    description: ->
      "#{@name}: #{dollarsToString(@balance)}"

    deposit: ({amount}) ->
      @balance += amount
      saveState()
      @

    withdraw: ({amount}) ->
      @balance -= amount
      saveState()
      @

    transfer: ({toAccount, amount}) ->
```

---

4.   https://github.com/jprichardson/node-jsonfile

```coffee
    @balance -= amount
    toAccount.balance += amount
    saveState()
    @
}
```

We're going to start with the same accounts as the original checkbooks, but unlike before, we're going to store them in an array:

Collections/checkbooks2/checkbooks2.coffee
```coffee
accounts = [
  createAccount({name: 'Checking'})
  createAccount({name: 'Savings'})
  createAccount({name: 'Mattress'})
]
```

Now for the tricky part: defining the interface. In the original checkbooks I tried to make this code as linear as possible, which worked reasonably well because our three prompts were always given in the same order: pick an account, pick an action, enter an amount. But the new "transfer" action requires a additional input (the destination account), which we'd like to prompt for before we prompt for the amount. Writing all of this logic in a linear fashion is still possible, but the resulting code wouldn't be much fun to read. So let's separate out the details—the parameters we pass to Inquirer.js to define each prompt—from the core application logic. This makes the core logic nice and easy to grok, with just two "steps" (one before an action is selected, and the other after):

Collections/checkbooks2/checkbooks2.coffee
```coffee
inquirer = require('inquirer')

mainStep = ->
  inquirer.prompt([
    makeAccountPrompt()
    makeActionPrompt()
  ], postActionStep)

postActionStep = ({account, action}) ->
  prompts = [makeAmountPrompt({action})]
  if action is 'transfer'
    prompts.unshift makeToAccountPrompt({fromAccount: account})
  inquirer.prompt(prompts, ({amount, toAccount}) ->
    amount = inputToNumber(amount)
    account[action]({amount, toAccount})
    mainStep()
  )
```

Once again, we're going heavy on object arguments so that we don't have to worry about the order of arguments. CoffeeScript's destructuring syntax really shines here.

And now for the prompt definitions:

Collections/checkbooks2/checkbooks2.coffee

```coffee
makeAccountPrompt = ->
  {
    name: 'account'
    message: 'Pick an account:'
    type: 'list'
    choices: for account in accounts
      {name: account.description(), value: account}
  }

makeActionPrompt = ->
  {
    name: 'action'
    message: 'Pick an action:'
    type: 'list'
    choices: [
      {name: 'Deposit $ into this account', value: 'deposit'}
      {name: 'Withdraw $ from this account', value: 'withdraw'}
      {name: 'Transfer $ to another account', value: 'transfer'}
    ]
  }

makeToAccountPrompt = ({fromAccount}) ->
  {
    name: 'toAccount'
    message: 'Pick an account to transfer $ to:'
    type: 'list'
    choices: for account in accounts when account isnt fromAccount
      {name: account.description(), value: account}
  }

makeAmountPrompt = ({action}) ->
  {
    name: 'amount'
    message: "Enter the amount to #{action}:"
    type: 'input'
    validate: (input) =>
      if isNaN(inputToNumber(input))
        return 'Please enter a numerical amount.'
      if inputToNumber(input) < 0
        return 'Please enter a non-negative amount.'
      true
  }
```

We need to define the same utility functions as in the original checkbooks, plus a new one to save the state of our accounts to a JSON file:

Collections/checkbooks2/checkbooks2.coffee

```
numeral = require ('numeral')
jsonfile = require('jsonfile')

dollarsToString = (dollars) ->
  numeral(dollars).format('$0,0.00')

inputToNumber = (input) ->
  parseFloat input.replace(/[$,]/g, ''), 10

saveState = ->
  jsonfile.writeFileSync('./data.json', accounts)
```

Now when we start the program, we try to load that JSON file and set the appropriate balance value for each account. Then we go to the main step:

Collections/checkbooks2/checkbooks2.coffee

```
try
  data = jsonfile.readFileSync('./data.json')
  for account, i in accounts
    account.balance = data[i].balance

mainStep()
```

Here's what it looks like in action:

```
$ coffee checkbooks2.coffee
[?] Pick an account: Checking: $0.00
[?] Pick an action: deposit
[?] Enter the amount to deposit: 1000000
[?] Pick an account: Checking: $1,000,000.00
[?] Pick an action: transfer
[?] Pick an account to transfer $ to: (Use arrow keys)
> Savings: $0.00
  Mattress: $0.00
```

Gotta Catch 'Em All

In this chapter, you learned how to use CoffeeScript syntax to manipulate JavaScript's two fundamental data structures: hash maps and arrays. You also learned how to iterate over those collections with loops and to use loops to create more collections.

In the next chapter, we'll deal with the most complex (and perhaps the most powerful) of all CoffeeScript features: classes.

## CHAPTER 4

Classes, Prototypes, and Inheritance

In the previous chapter, you learned to create and manipulate objects. But we don't yet have a way of defining *types* of objects. In JavaScript, types are described by *prototypes*, which define methods (and, less often, data) that can be shared across many objects. For that reason, JavaScript is sometimes described as a prototype-based language.

This dynamic approach to sharing methods is powerful but has a cost in clarity. If you're reading code in a strictly class-based language like C++ or Java and you want to find out which methods a particular object supports, you just have to look at the code that defines that object's class. But if you want to know which methods a JavaScript object has (without running the code), you have to track down every possible reference to that object or its prototype anywhere in the application.

Several approaches have popped up over the years for organizing JavaScript code into something resembling classes. Over time, a standard pattern evolved. That pattern provides the basis for CoffeeScript's classes, which preserve the dynamism of prototypes while greatly simplifying the task of defining new types of objects. In this chapter, we'll review the mechanics of JavaScript prototypes, then meet CoffeeScript's two most powerful keywords: class and extends.

The Power of Prototypes

A prototype is an object whose properties are shared by all objects that have that prototype. An object's prototype can usually be accessed using the aptly named prototype property, though there are exceptions.[1]

---

1. http://javascriptweblog.wordpress.com/2010/06/07/understanding-javascript-prototypes/

However, you can't just go and write A.prototype = B. Instead, you need to use the new keyword, which takes a function and creates an object that "inherits" that function's prototype. When a function is used this way, it's referred to as a *constructor*. Here's a quick example:

```
Boy = ->          # by convention, constructor names are capitalized
Boy::sing = ->
  console.log "It ain't easy being a boy named Sue"
sue = new Boy()
sue.sing()
```

Here, Boy::sing is shorthand for Boy.prototype.sing. The :: symbol is to prototype as @ is to this.

The output looks like this:

```
It ain't easy being a boy named Sue
```

Cool, right? Let's learn more about what constructors can do.

Making Objects with Constructors

When we write new <constructor>, several things happen: a new object is created, that object is given the prototype from the constructor, and the constructor is executed (in the new object's context). So let's say we want to define a "gift" type, where every new gift stores the name passed to the constructor and announces the existing number of gifts:

```
Classes/gift.coffee
Gift = (@name) ->
  Gift.count++
  @day = Gift.count
  @announce()

Gift.count = 0
Gift::announce = ->
  console.log "On day #{@day} of Christmas I received #{@name}"

gift1 = new Gift('a partridge in a pear tree')
gift2 = new Gift('two turtle doves')
```

The syntax (@name) -> is a handy shorthand for (name) -> @name = name. Here's the output:

```
On day 1 of Christmas I received a partridge in a pear tree
On day 2 of Christmas I received two turtle doves
```

Each time the Gift constructor runs, it does four things: assigns the given name to @name (using the argument shorthand), increments the count property on the Gift constructor, copies that value to @day, and runs the @announce function inherited from the prototype.

Notice that all of the functions on the new object run in the context of the object. Prototypes are the reason why the this keyword, as odd as it may seem, is essential to the JavaScript language. Prototypes allow a single function to be shared across many objects, and this allows shared functions to access the state of different objects depending on how they're called.

When it comes to parentheses, constructors have some syntactic quirks to watch out for:

1. When you invoke a constructor with no arguments, you can omit the parentheses. So new Date and new Date() are equivalent.

2. Parentheses do, however, matter when you invoke a constructor that's attached to an object: new x.Y() creates a new instance of x.Y, while new X().y instantiates X and returns its y property.

3. When you omit the parentheses, they implicitly go at the end: new x.Y is equivalent to new x.Y().

CoffeeScript gets a lot of guff from some corners for its implicit parentheses, but these rules come from pure JavaScript.

Prototype Precedence

When an object inherits properties from a prototype, changes to the prototype will change the inherited properties as well:

Classes/raven.coffee
```
Raven = ->
Raven::quoth = -> console.log 'Nevermore'
raven1 = new Raven
raven1.quoth()    # Nevermore

Raven::quoth = -> console.log "I'm hungry"
raven1.quoth()    # I'm hungry
```

Properties attached directly to objects take precedence over prototype properties. So we can remove that ambiguity by writing this:

Classes/raven.coffee
```
raven2 = new Raven
raven2.quoth = -> console.log "I'm my own kind of raven"
raven1.quoth()    # I'm hungry
raven2.quoth()    # I'm my own kind of raven
```

To check whether a property is attached to an object directly or inherited from a prototype, use the hasOwnProperty function:

Classes/raven.coffee
```
console.log raven1.hasOwnProperty('quoth')  # false
console.log raven2.hasOwnProperty('quoth')  # true
```

I should mention one interesting syntactical implication. The statement obj.a = obj.a is not always a no-op:

Classes/raven.coffee
```
raven3 = new Raven
console.log raven3.hasOwnProperty('quoth')  # false
raven3.quoth = raven3.quoth
console.log raven3.hasOwnProperty('quoth')  # true
```

All of this prototype manipulation is well and good, but it's a bit messy, isn't it? Shouldn't there be a clearer way of distinguishing constructor properties (such as Gift.count) from prototype properties (such as Gift::announce)? And of distinguishing constructors from other functions? That's exactly what Coffee-Script's class keyword allows us to do.

Classes: Giving Prototypes Structure

To reap the benefits of prototypal inheritance in JavaScript, you have to define a constructor and then attach properties to its associated prototype. Coffee-Script allows you to do both of those things at once using the class keyword:

```
class MyFirstClass
  sayHello: -> console.log "Hello, I'm a class!"

myFirstInstance = new MyFirstClass
myFirstInstance.sayHello()

Hello, I'm a class!
```

In just two lines, we've defined a no-op constructor named MyFirstClass and attached a method called sayHello to its prototype. Of course, we could do that in two lines without the class keyword. So let's look at a more involved example.

It's a well-known fact that the trouble a tribble makes is directly proportional to the number of existing tribbles. Let's write a class that demonstrates that wisdom:

Classes/tribble.coffee
```
class Tribble
  constructor: ->
    @isAlive = true
    Tribble.count += 1
```

```
# Prototype properties
breed: -> new Tribble if @isAlive
die: ->
  return unless @isAlive
  Tribble.count -= 1
  @isAlive = false

# Class-level properties
@count: 0
@makeTrouble: -> console.log ('Trouble!' for i in [1..@count]).join(' ')
```

There's a lot of new syntax here, so let's go through it one piece at a time.

Each time a new tribble is created, the constructor method runs. (This syntax reflects JavaScript semantics: for any function X, X.prototype.constructor is X.) The constructor sets the isAlive property on the new instance to true and then bumps Tribble.count up by one.

A tribble has two prototypal methods: one to spawn new tribbles and another to remove itself from the population. It's perfectly kosher to reference the constructor (in this case, Tribble) from prototypal methods, because the constructor will always be defined before they're called.

In the class body, @ points to the constructor rather than the prototype, and you can define "static" (class-level) properties with the special syntax @key: value (which is equivalent to @key = value). So we're initializing Tribble.count to be 0 and defining a Tribble.makeTrouble() function. Making count a class-level property rather than a prototype-level one avoids any potential ambiguity over whether an instance's count is specific to that instance or shared.

Let's test this:

Classes/tribble.coffee
```
tribble1 = new Tribble
tribble2 = new Tribble
Tribble.makeTrouble()    # "Trouble! Trouble!"
```

Trouble! Trouble!

By instantiating two tribbles, we've bolstered Tribble.count to two, so Tribble.makeTrouble's loop for i in [1..@count] has two iterations. Let's see if we can bring the count back down:

Classes/tribble.coffee
```
tribble1.die()
Tribble.makeTrouble()    # "Trouble!"
```

Trouble!

Killing off tribble1 again would have no effect, thanks to the unless @isAlive check. And as we know, tribbles are born pregnant, so it won't be long before the remaining individual repopulates the species:

Classes/tribble.coffee
```
tribble2.breed().breed().breed()
Tribble.makeTrouble()    # "Trouble! Trouble! Trouble! Trouble!"
```

```
Trouble! Trouble! Trouble! Trouble!
```

That covers the basics of the class syntax. But much like tribbles, classes are famous for replicating themselves. So let's close this chapter by introducing the best part of CoffeeScript classes: inheritance.

Inheritance: Classy Prototype Chains

You've seen how prototypes allow a set of objects to share common functionality and how CoffeeScript's classes provide a useful syntax for bundling prototype properties together. And if that were all classes did, they'd be fairly useful. But where classes really shine is when we want to share properties between objects with distinct but related types, a process called *inheritance.*

JavaScript supports inheritance through something called "prototype chains." Let's say that C's prototype, B, has its own prototype, A. Then we write this:

```
c = new C
console.log c.flurb()
```

First, the runtime checks to see whether the particular C instance, c, has a property flurb; if not, it checks C's prototype (B). If that's still no dice, it checks B's prototype (A). In short, it's traversing the prototype chain.

What happens if A has no flurb, either? Then the runtime checks the default object prototype (that is, the prototype of {}). So, every prototype inherits from {}'s prototype, but there may be other prototypes in between.

All of this assigning prototypes to prototypes to prototypes can get a little messy. That's where CoffeeScript's extends keyword comes in:

```
class B extends A
```

Here, B's prototype will inherit from A's prototype. In addition, A's class-level properties are copied over (shallowly) to B. So if we left the definition of B alone, B instances would have exactly the same behavior as A instances. (There is one exception: B.name would be 'B' while A.name would be 'A', because name is a special property for JavaScript functions.)

Now let's look at a slightly more complex example that takes advantage of another keyword, super:

```
class Pet
  constructor: -> @isHungry = true
  eat: -> @isHungry = false

class Dog extends Pet
  eat: ->
    console.log '*crunch, crunch*'
    super()
  fetch: ->
    console.log 'Yip yip!'
    @isHungry = true
```

The constructor from Pet is inherited by Dog, which means that dogs start out hungry. When a dog eats, it makes some noises and then invokes super(), which means "call the method of the same name on the parent class." (More precisely, it means Pet::eat.call this.) Then the dog is no longer hungry.

If a constructor is defined on the child class, then it overrides the constructor from the parent class. It can invoke the parent constructor at any time using super(). It's usually wise to call super() (or, more likely, super—see the following sidebar) at the start of a subclass constructor.

The super Keyword and Arguments

What's wrong with this code?

```
class Appliance
  constructor: (warranty) ->
    warrantyDb.save(this) if warranty

class Toaster extends Appliance
  constructor: (warranty) ->
    super()
```

When we create a new Toaster, super() will invoke the parent constructor without passing along the warranty argument, which means that the toaster won't be saved in the warranty database.

We could fix this by writing super(warranty), but there's a shorthand we can use instead: super. With no parentheses or arguments, super will pass on every one of the current function's arguments. If you're a Rubyist, this will seem familiar. If not, just think of super as a greedy keyword: if you don't tell it which arguments you want it to pass along, it'll take 'em all.

Believe it or not, you now know everything there is to know about classes. As with everything in CoffeeScript, the syntax may be distant from JavaScript, but the translation is straightforward. If you're a fan of classical OOP (object-oriented programming) methodology, this next section's for you.

Polymorphism and Switching

One great use of classes is *polymorphism*, which is a fancy object-oriented programming term for "a thing can be a lot of different things, but not just *any* thing." Here's a classic example:

```
class Shape
  constructor: (@width) ->
  computeArea: -> throw new Error('I am an abstract class!')

class Square extends Shape
  computeArea: -> Math.pow @width, 2

class Circle extends Shape
  radius: -> @width / 2
  computeArea: -> Math.PI * Math.pow @radius(), 2

showArea = (shape) ->
  unless shape instanceof Shape
    throw new Error('showArea requires a Shape instance!')
  console.log shape.computeArea()

showArea new Square(2)   # 4
showArea new Circle(2)   # pi
```

Notice that the showArea function checks that the object passed to it is a Shape instance (using the instanceof keyword). But it doesn't care what kind of shape it's been given; both Square and Circle instances will work. While this is a trivial example, it's not hard to imagine a rich geometry library that takes this approach.

If we didn't use the instanceof check, that would be known as "duck typing" (as in, "If it looks like a duck..."). If the target object doesn't have a computeArea function, then we'll get a meaningful error message anyway. Duck typing is great, but there are times when you want to be sure that a particular object is what you think it is.

A common idiom in more classic object-oriented languages is to use polymorphism with switch. We haven't talked about CoffeeScript's switch yet, and there are a couple of important differences between it and JavaScript's switch. First, there's an implicit break between clauses to prevent unintended "fallthrough"; second, the result of the switch is returned. (When the return value is used, break and return are not allowed. If you try, you'll get SyntaxError: cannot include a pure statement in an expression. That's the compiler's way of telling you that it doesn't make sense to write a = return x.)

CoffeeScript also makes several syntactic changes, in part to remind JavaScripters of these hidden differences: when is used instead of case, and else instead of default. (The keywords are borrowed from Ruby, where the case structure has similar semantics.) A single when can be followed by several potential matches, delimited by commas. Also, instead of :, those match clauses are separated from their outcomes by indentation (or then).

Here's how it all comes together in a simple factory function:

```coffee
requisitionStarship = (captain) ->
  switch captain
    when 'Kirk', 'Picard', 'Archer'
      new Enterprise()
    when 'Janeway'
      new Voyager()
    else
      throw new Error('Invalid starship captain')
```

Mini-Project: All-Purpose Checkbook Balancer

By now, I assume you've abandoned Mint.com and embraced the checkbook balancer that we've built over the last two chapters. But there's one feature that you might miss: the ability to track additional accounts beyond checking, savings, and your mattress. For the final version of the checkbook balancer, we're going to add the ability to add and remove accounts. We're also going refactor our code into classes (and into more than one file!), making it easier to think of the program in terms of separate, reasonably decoupled components.

Let's start by installing our dependencies, which will be the same as in checkbooks2:

```
$ npm init
$ npm install --save inquirer
$ npm install --save numeral
$ npm install --save jsonfile
```

We're going to have a reasonably concise checkbooks3.coffee, containing only our application's core logic, by require-ing three other project modules that we're going to define separately.

(The code listing is on the next page.)

Classes/checkbooks3/checkbooks3.coffee

```coffee
inquirer = require('inquirer')

Account = require('./account')
PromptFactory = require('./promptFactory')
utils = require('./utils')

# Define our logic for each prompt the user can reach
promptFactory = new PromptFactory({allAccounts: Account.allAccounts})

mainStep = ->
  inquirer.prompt promptFactory.accountPrompt(), ({account}) ->
    if account is null
      createAccountStep()
    else
      actionStep({account})

createAccountStep = ->
  inquirer.prompt promptFactory.newAccountPrompt(), ({name}) ->
    new Account({balance: 0, name})
    Account.saveState()
    mainStep()

actionStep = ({account}) ->
  inquirer.prompt promptFactory.actionPrompt({account}), ({action}) ->
    postActionStep({account, action})

postActionStep = ({account, action}) ->
  prompts = [promptFactory.amountPrompt({action})]
  if action is 'transfer'
    prompts.unshift promptFactory.toAccountPrompt({fromAccount: account})

  inquirer.prompt prompts, ({amount, toAccount}) ->
    amount = utils.inputToNumber(amount)
    account[action]({amount, toAccount})
    mainStep()

# Load data
Account.loadState()

# Show the first prompt
mainStep()
```

I've capitalized Account and PromptFactory because these are class names. The new Account class is an amalgam of the old createAccount function and our persistence logic:

Classes/checkbooks3/account.coffee

```coffee
jsonfile = require('jsonfile')

utils = require('./utils')

# Account implements all actions that affect data

class Account
  constructor: ({@name, @balance}) ->
    Account.allAccounts.push @
    return

  description: ->
    "#{@name}: #{utils.dollarsToString(@balance)}"

  deposit: ({amount}) ->
    @balance += amount
    Account.saveState()
    @

  withdraw: ({amount}) ->
    @balance -= amount
    Account.saveState()
    @

  transfer: ({toAccount, amount}) ->
    @balance -= amount
    toAccount.balance += amount
    Account.saveState()
    @

  @allAccounts = []

  @saveState: ->
    jsonfile.writeFileSync('./data.json', Account.allAccounts)

  @loadState: ->
    try
      Account.allAccounts = for accountData in jsonfile.readFileSync('./data.json')
        new Account(accountData)
    catch e
      Account.allAccounts = [
        new Account({balance: 0, name: 'checking'})
        new Account({balance: 0, name: 'savings'})
        new Account({balance: 0, name: 'mattress'})
      ]
    return

module.exports = Account
```

Some of our prompts require the data now stored as Account.allAccounts. We don't want to create a global, but we also don't want the repetition of passing that data every time we call a prompt function. So, I've attached those prompt functions as methods on a class called PromptFactory, which takes an array of accounts in its constructor and stores the reference:

Classes/checkbooks3/promptFactory.coffee

```coffee
utils = require('./utils')

# PromptFactory defines the presentation of each prompt in the app

class PromptFactory
  constructor: ({@allAccounts}) ->

  accountPrompt: ->
    {
      name: 'account'
      message: 'Pick an account:'
      type: 'list'
      choices: (for account in @allAccounts
        {name: account.description(), value: account}
      ).concat({name: 'new account', value: null})
    }

  newAccountPrompt: ->
    {
      name: 'name'
      message: 'Enter a name for this account:'
      type: 'input'
      validate: (input) =>
        for account in @allAccounts
          if account.name is input
            return 'That account name is already taken!'
        true
    }

  actionPrompt: ({account}) ->
    {
      name: 'action'
      message: 'Pick an action:'
      type: 'list'
      choices: [
        {name: 'Deposit $ into this account', value: 'deposit'}
        {name: 'Withdraw $ from this account', value: 'withdraw'}
        {name: 'Transfer $ to another account', value: 'transfer'}
      ]
    }

  toAccountPrompt: ({fromAccount}) ->
    {
```

```
      name: 'toAccount'
      message: 'Pick an account to transfer $ to:'
      type: 'list'
      choices: for account in @allAccounts when account isnt fromAccount
        {name: account.description(), value: account}
    }

  amountPrompt: ({action}) ->
    {
      name: 'amount'
      message: "Enter the amount to #{action}:"
      type: 'input'
      validate: (input) =>
        if isNaN(utils.inputToNumber(input))
          return 'Please enter a numerical amount.'
        if utils.inputToNumber(input) < 0
          return 'Please enter a non-negative amount.'
        true
    }

module.exports = PromptFactory
```

All that's left is our utility functions, which now reside in their own handy
file of miscellany:

Classes/checkbooks3/utils.coffee
```
numeral = require ('numeral')

# Utility functions

module.exports =
  dollarsToString: (dollars) ->
    numeral(dollars).format('$0,0.00')

  inputToNumber: (input) ->
    parseFloat input.replace(/[$,]/g, ''), 10
```

And here's what our final, feature-packed iteration of the checkbook balancer
looks like:

$ coffee checkbooks3.coffee
```
[?] Pick an account: (Use arrow keys)
> checking: $22.00
  savings: -$5.00
  mattress: $0.00
  money market: $5.00
  hedge fund: $9,999.00
  new account
```

Just a Spoonful of Sugar

That's it for our coverage of classes. Just remember: CoffeeScript doesn't require you to use classes or classic object-oriented design patterns—most JavaScript developers do perfectly fine without either—but for some applications, classes are a natural fit.

For the rest of the book, you'll take what you've learned about the CoffeeScript language and use it to develop a working web application. We'll start with the front end, using two of the most popular frameworks in web development today: jQuery and Backbone.

CHAPTER 5

Web Applications with
jQuery and Backbone.js

JavaScript was born in the browser. From its birth in 1995 to the turn of the century, it was primarily used to "enhance" websites with special effects and clunky interactive features, often to their detriment. But JavaScript in the browser came into its own as a software development platform when Google launched Gmail, proving that a practical and feature-rich application could live on the Web with no need for Flash or other proprietary plugins.

Gmail's success inspired intense interest in the Web as an app platform, but developers were stymied by the browser's clunky APIs, made worse by inconsistencies (often undocumented) from one browser to another. Then, in 2006, 22-year-old John Resig launched jQuery, an open-source library that abstracted away many of the browsers' problems and introduced an ingenious CSS-like element selection syntax. Today, jQuery is used by nearly one-third of the 10,000 most-visited websites.[1] Although browser APIs have become dramatically better and more standardized since jQuery's initial release, the case for using jQuery remains strong. It works around hundreds of browser bugs, with only a small performance penalty.

As web applications have grown more complex, numerous MVC (Model-View-Controller) frameworks have cropped up to provide organizational structure. Of these, the most popular is Backbone.js, written primarily by CoffeeScript creator Jeremy Ashkenas. Backbone is a relatively minimal framework, making it suitable to a wide range of applications. Additionally, Backbone

---

1.   http://trends.builtwith.com/javascript/JQuery

uses classes that are intercompatible with CoffeeScript classes, making it an especially strong choice for CoffeeScripters.

In this chapter, you'll learn the basics of jQuery and Backbone.js as you build the first iteration of CoffeeTasks, a Trello-like task management application. (Trello is an infinitely more full-featured application than the one you'll be writing in this chapter, but it uses many of the same technologies—including CoffeeScript.[2]) Going into great detail about these handy libraries would be beyond the scope of this book, so I encourage you to jump from this chapter into the (excellent) official docs[3] if you get stuck at any point.

Building the Project with Grunt

Before we dive into our project's code, we need to solve a problem: browsers don't understand CoffeeScript. And they don't understand Eco, the templating language you'll meet a bit later. They only understand JavaScript. So how do we turn our source files into JavaScript with minimal pain and frustration?

The answer is Grunt.[4] Grunt is a Node.js-based task runner, well-suited to compiling our project assets (Eco templates and CoffeeScript modules) into JavaScript. In fact, it already has plugins that tell it how to do those exact things!

Let's start by setting up our project directory:

```
$ mkdir coffee-tasks
$ cd coffee-tasks
$ npm init
```

npm will give you a series of prompts, which will fill in the project's initial package.json. Now we can use npm to install Grunt and the plugins we need, while saving those dependencies to package.json in case we need to reinstall them later:

```
$ npm install -g grunt-cli
$ npm install --save-dev grunt
$ npm install --save-dev grunt-eco
$ npm install --save-dev grunt-contrib-coffee
$ npm install --save-dev grunt-contrib-watch
```

Careful readers will notice that we just installed Grunt twice. Actually, this is a quirk of how Grunt works: to get a grunt command we can run directly, we need to install Grunt globally. Hence, -g for "global." But wait—what if we

---

2. http://blog.fogcreek.com/the-trello-tech-stack/
3. jQuery: http://api.jquery.com and Backbone: http://backbonejs.org/
4. http://gruntjs.com/

Grunt vs. Gulp

In the early days of Node, it was clear that a plugin-based build tool was needed. Grunt, first released in early 2012, was the first to achieve widespread adoption. But it soon faced serious competition from another build tool, Gulp.

The decision on whether to use Grunt or Gulp has stymied many Node developers. Gulp is more versatile in theory, but for most projects, either tool will do just fine. I chose Grunt for this book for the simple reason that as of this writing it's more widely used.

If you'd like to learn more about the differences between the two, I recommend Mark Dalgleish's "Build Wars" presentation.[a]

a.   http://markdalgleish.github.io/presentation-build-wars-gulp-vs-grunt/

had multiple projects on the same machine that required different versions of Grunt? The designers of Grunt came up with a clever solution for this all-too-common software headache: when you install Grunt globally, what you're really installing is just a thin wrapper (called grunt-cli) that loads the grunt package from the local project. That way, every project can have its own Grunt, despite sharing the same grunt command!

Now we have all the npm packages we need for our Gruntfile. This is the file that Grunt looks for every time we run it. It tells Grunt which files it needs to compile and where to put the results of that compilation. Oh, and we can write it in CoffeeScript:

jQuery/Gruntfile.coffee
```
module.exports = (grunt) ->
  grunt.loadNpmTasks('grunt-eco')
  grunt.loadNpmTasks('grunt-contrib-watch')
  grunt.loadNpmTasks('grunt-contrib-coffee')

  grunt.initConfig
    watch:
      coffee:
        files: 'src/*.coffee'
        tasks: ['coffee:compile']
      eco:
        files: 'templates/*.eco'
        tasks: ['eco:compile']

    coffee:
      compile:
        expand: true
        flatten: true
```

```
    options:
      sourceMap: true
    cwd: 'src/'
    src: ['*.coffee']
    dest: 'compiled/'
    ext: '.js'

eco:
  compile:
    src: 'templates/*.eco'
    dest: 'compiled/templates.js'

grunt.registerTask('build', ['coffee', 'eco'])
grunt.registerTask('default', ['build', 'watch'])
```

This file does three things:

1. Compiles our CoffeeScript files from the src directory into the compiled directory. (Because we specified the sourceMap: true option, we'll also get a .js.map file alongside each compiled .js file.)

2. Compiles our Eco files from the templates directory into the compiled directory.

3. Watches those CoffeeScript and Eco files and recompiles them whenever they change.

This is an ideal setup for local development, so I've made this the default task. That means that all we have to do to kick things off is:

```
$ grunt
```

Grunt is an enormously flexible tool. If we were preparing our project for production, we could also use Grunt to concatenate our JS, run tests, and perhaps even deploy our files to staging and production. For more information on Grunt, check out *Automate with Grunt [Hog14]* from The Pragmatic Bookshelf.

Managing Front-End Dependencies with Bower

As I mentioned at the start of the chapter (and, for that matter, in its title), we're going to use jQuery and Backbone.js in this project. So how do we include those dependencies? It seems like only yesterday that developers were manually downloading JavaScript libraries from the Web. Well, okay, that's still common. But it's not nearly as common as it was, thanks to front-end package managers inspired by npm—most notably Bower.

With Bower, we can install JavaScript libraries for web applications via the command line, keep those libraries up to date, and automatically ensure that their dependencies are met. For example, Backbone relies on Underscore, so when we use Bower to install Backbone, Bower grabs Underscore for us automatically!

There isn't that much more to say about Bower. It's a nice, simple utility with an interface closely modeled on npm's. Conveniently, Bower is itself installable with npm:

```
$ npm install -g bower
```

Once installed, Bower can prepare any project for front-end dependency management with its equivalent of npm init:

```
$ bower init
```

Go through the prompts, and you'll end up with a bower.json file (analogous to npm's package.json), which lets Bower keep track of your project's dependencies. Now let's install those dependencies:

```
$ bower install --save jquery
$ bower install --save backbone
```

Done! Now, unlike JavaScript dependency libraries such as AMD, Bower doesn't tell us how to load the dependencies it installs. This means we just need to give our page script tags pointing at the right files—most likely before our own scripts. Below, I'm going to give you the complete index.html for our entire project. Apologies for any spoilers:

jQuery/index.html
```
<!DOCTYPE html>
<html>
<head>
  <title>CoffeeTasks</title>

  <!-- Libraries -->
  <script src="bower_components/jquery/dist/jquery.js"></script>
  <script src="bower_components/underscore/underscore.js"></script>
  <script src="bower_components/backbone/backbone.js"></script>

  <!-- Default data -->
  <script src="compiled/data.js"></script>

  <!-- Templates -->
  <script src="compiled/templates.js"></script>

  <!-- Backbone models/views -->
  <script src="compiled/card.js"></script>
  <script src="compiled/column.js"></script>
  <script src="compiled/board.js"></script>
```

```
  <!-- Application core -->
  <script src="compiled/application.js"></script>

  <!-- Stylesheets -->
  <link rel="stylesheet" href="css/normalize.css">
  <link rel="stylesheet" href="css/style.css">
</head>
<body>
  <!-- All content is rendered client-side -->
</body>
</html>
```

The rest of this chapter will be devoted to the real nuts and bolts of our application: templates, models, and views.

Building the Page with Templates

Nothing is more fundamental to a web application than how it generates the HTML that ultimately tells the browser what to display, and nothing generates more heated arguments among web application developers. A bevy of templating libraries allow empty shells of HTML to be filled with specific content, ranging from the trivial (Underscore.js's _.template function) to the extravagant (React.js/JSX). Even the choice between generating HTML on the server or on the client is wrought with controversy: client-side rendering is sleek, but server-side rendering is enormously flexible, as it can handle an unlimited number of special cases (personalization, internationalization, errors, and security checks...) without passing on the weight of that code to the browser.

All this controversy is beyond the scope of this book. You're here to learn CoffeeScript! So for this project, we're going to use a templating language called Eco.[5] Eco allows you to write templates that look like HTML with CoffeeScript snippets thrown in for conditionals and loops. Eco can be rendered on the server, but we'll stick to client-side rendering so that we don't have to write a Node server until the next chapter. (In the real world, client-side rendering might be preferred for an application like this one so that it can run offline and then sync changes to the server later.)

Now let's figure out what templates we need. For simplicity, we'll have a 1:1 correspondence between templates and Backbone views, and a 1:1 correspondence between Backbone views and Backbone models. So what kinds of entities will our task manager have? I'm thinking:

---

5. https://github.com/sstephenson/eco/

- A board, with a name and a number of columns to group task cards
- A column, with a name and containing any number of task cards
- A task card, with a description and a due date

That's all we need for our simple app. So let's turn those descriptions into markup:

```
jQuery/templates/board.eco
<input name='board-name' value='<%= @name %>'>
<div class='column-container'>
  <% for column in @columns : %>
    <div class='column' data-column-id='<%= column.id %>'></div>
  <% end %>
  <button name='add-column'>Add Column</button>
</div>
```

```
jQuery/templates/column.eco
<input name='column-name' value='<%= @name %>'>
<div class='card-container'>
  <% for card in @cards : %>
    <div class='card' data-card-id='<%= card.id %>'></div>
  <% end %>
  <button name='add-card'>Add Card</button>
</div>
```

```
jQuery/templates/card.eco
<textarea name='card-description' placeholder='Description'
  rows='3'><%= @description %></textarea>
<label class='due-date-label'><span>Due by:</span><input type='date'
  name='due-date' value='<%= @dueDate %>'></label>
```

We're not asking the templating library to pull much weight in this application. All it has to do is be better than putting your templates directly in your JavaScript code as strings and loops. In addition to being more fun to write, the templating library serves an important security function by escaping all strings before they're inserted into the DOM. The syntax <%= value %> replaces HTML characters like > and < with codes like > and < that display as those characters. In a multi-user application, this becomes extremely important. Without escaping, one user could insert a <script> tag into a card that could, when viewed by another user, send him that user's login cookie!

Note that we're relying on one fairly cutting-edge browser feature here: the date input type. In a production application, we'd want to use a JavaScript library to power our datepicker. But since you're a developer, I'm going to trust that your browser is up to date (no pun intended), allowing our project to have minimal dependencies.

Now, using the power of Backbone, we're going to bring this markup to life.

Structuring Data for Persistence

All good apps are built around data. In our case, the data in our app is going to be used to fill in the templates from the previous section. Before we start thinking about how to represent this data in Backbone, we should figure out a reasonable schema for persisting it as JSON on the back end.

We're going to use a relational schema: the user will have an array of boards, an array of columns, and an array of cards. So a user with one of each entity would have a dataset that looks something like this:

```
{
  "boards": [
    {
      "id": 1,
      "name": "Pet Tasks",
      "columnIds": [1]
    }
  ],
  "columns": [
    {
      "id": 1,
      "name": "Dog Tasks",
      "cardIds": [1]
    }
  ],
  "cards": [
    {
      "id": 1,
      "description": "Walk the dog",
      "dueDate": "2015-12-25"
    }
  ]
}
```

You might wonder, why not use a nested, nonrelational schema? Card data could be nested inside of column data, which in turn could be nested inside of board data. Since columns are never shared across boards and cards are never shared across boards, such a scheme would be workable for this very small project. However, it would be extremely brittle if we decided to add new features, such as cards that live outside of columns. Worse, it would be a scalability nightmare: sooner or later, we would have to figure out a way to avoid loading a user's entire dataset into the browser when the user loads the page, which would force us to use a different schema on the client than the one used in the database and then write code to map between the two. A relational schema makes that problem trivial (at least on the front end) by allowing us to load any subset of boards and then load only the columns associated with those boards and the cards associated with those columns.

With our schema in place, we're ready to design the corresponding Backbone entity classes.

Representing Data in Backbone Models and Collections

A *model*, in the Backbone sense, is an entity that serves as a key-value store where changes can be observed via event listeners. Additionally, Backbone models inherit methods for syncing their data with a remote server. That's all there is to it, and yet models are the heart of Backbone. Being able to "listen" for changes to a set of data is incredibly powerful: change events can tell us when we need to re-render a view, display a message, or fetch additional data. Before Backbone, most JavaScript applications had no model layer. They performed actions in direct response to user input events, making it very difficult to maintain a consistent application state. Separating out the view and model layers was an enormous leap forward for client-side application development, and it's fair to say that Backbone was pivotal in popularizing this approach.

Backbone also defines *collections*, ordered sets of models that can also be observed via event listeners. When we load our data from the server (or, for this chapter, from localStorage), we're going to load each of the three arrays into a corresponding collection: one for boards, one for columns, and one for cards. We'll start with the cards, because they contain no references to other types. Here is our card model class and the corresponding collection class, both of which we're attaching to window as we define them so that they're visible to other modules:

jQuery/src/card.coffee
```
class window.Card extends Backbone.Model
```

jQuery/src/card.coffee
```
class window.CardCollection extends Backbone.Collection
  model: Card
```

Simple? Very. We haven't added any functionality to the underlying Backbone.Model and Backbone.Collection classes. In a normal application, we'd at least add a url property to point to a RESTful API endpoint. But that's a feat we'll save for the next chapter. Instead, we're going to modify Backbone to persist data with localStorage. To do that, we'll override Backbone.sync, which provides the persistence functionality underlying every model and collection's save and fetch methods. More on that in a bit.

Before we can load our columns, we need to load our cards so that each column's cardIds have cards to point to. So we'll define a global collection and load all of the cards in localStorage into it:

jQuery/src/card.coffee
```coffee
cardData = JSON.parse(localStorage.cards)
window.allCards = new CardCollection(cardData, {parse: true})
```

Now on to the Column model. Because of cardIds, this is going to be slightly more complicated than the Card model. We're going to implement parse and toJSON methods, which Backbone uses to convert raw JSON data into the model's attributes and vice versa:

jQuery/src/column.coffee
```coffee
class window.Column extends Backbone.Model
  defaults:
    name: 'New Column'

  parse: (data) ->
    attrs = _.omit data, 'cardIds'

    # Convert the raw cardIds array into a collection
    attrs.cards = @get('cards') ? new window.CardCollection
    attrs.cards.reset(
      for cardId in data.cardIds or []
        window.allCards.get(cardId)
    )

    attrs

  toJSON: ->
    data = _.omit @attributes, 'cards'

    # Convert the cards collection into a cardIds array
    data.cardIds = @get('cards').pluck 'id'

    data
```

Let's break down the parse method:

First, we're using Underscore's _.omit method to make a shallow copy of the raw JSON data that exclude cardIds. When this copy is returned by parse, it's going to be used as the model's attributes. We're excluding cardIds because we don't want that array to become a part of the model; we want the cards referenced by that array instead. Having both would cause unnecessary data duplication and possible inconsistencies.

Second, we're creating a CardCollection that contains the models returned by a list comprehension. The list comprehension goes through cardIds and, for each unique ID, gets the card with that id from allCards.

The toJSON method simply does the opposite of what parse did, extracting the IDs from the column's CardCollection. The data we return from toJSON will be persisted to localStorage, perhaps to be passed into some new column's parse method one day.

We don't have to do any work for ColumnCollection. That's because when we instantiate a Backbone collection with a bunch of raw data, it automatically creates new models and calls the parse method on each one:

jQuery/src/column.coffee
```
class window.ColumnCollection extends Backbone.Collection
  model: Column
```

Now we can load all our columns from localStorage, just as we did with allCards:

jQuery/src/column.coffee
```
columnData = JSON.parse(localStorage.columns)
window.allColumns = new ColumnCollection(columnData, {parse: true})
```

The only model left to define is a board, which we define in much the same way that we defined a column:

jQuery/src/board.coffee
```
class window.Board extends Backbone.Model
  defaults:
    name: 'New Board'

  parse: (data) ->
    attrs = _.omit data, 'columnIds'

    # Convert the raw columnIds array into a collection
    attrs.columns = @get('columns') ? new window.ColumnCollection
    attrs.columns.reset(
      for columnId in data.columnIds or []
        window.allColumns.get(columnId)
    )

    attrs

  toJSON: ->
    data = _.omit @attributes, 'columns'

    # Convert the columns collection into a columnIds array
    data.columnIds = @get('columns').pluck 'id'

    data
```

```
class window.BoardCollection extends Backbone.Collection
  model: Board

boardData = JSON.parse(localStorage.boards)
window.allBoards = new BoardCollection(boardData, {parse: true})
```

Now we have all of our models and collections in place. However, we still need to write the logic needed to sync them with localStorage. That logic is very specific to this application, but I'll include it here for completeness' sake:

jQuery/src/application.coffee
```
Backbone.sync = (method, model, options) ->
  # We only have to handle model syncs (not collection syncs)
  if model instanceof window.Card
    collection = window.allCards
    localStorageKey = 'cards'
  else if model instanceof window.Column
    collection = window.allColumns
    localStorageKey ='columns'
  else if model instanceof window.Board
    collection = window.allBoards
    localStorageKey = 'boards'

  switch method
    when 'get'             # 'get' corresponds to a model.fetch() call
      model.reset collection.get(model.id), {silent: true}
    when 'create'          # 'create' is a model.save() call on a new model
      model.set 'id', collection.length + 1
      collection.add(model)
      localStorage[localStorageKey] = JSON.stringify collection.toJSON()
    when 'update'          # 'update' is a model.save() call on an old model
      localStorage[localStorageKey] = JSON.stringify collection.toJSON()

  # Simulate a successful jqXHR
  xhr = options.xhr = jQuery.Deferred().resolve(model.toJSON()).promise()
  options.success(model.toJSON())
  xhr
```

Don't worry if you're not sure how this sync logic works. Normal, server-driven applications don't usually have to muck with Backbone's internals this way. We'll get rid of this code in the next chapter, when we build a server for our application to sync to.

And that's it! The model layer of our application is complete. We've created three models (Card, Column, and Board) with corresponding collections and implemented the logic needed to persist them in the browser's localStorage. Now we just need to add a view layer that ties our models together with our templates, and we'll be ready to fire up our application.

Presenting Data with Views

A Backbone view is a do-it-yourself kit for turning a model into HTML. Unlike other JavaScript frameworks, Backbone doesn't perform rendering or respond to input events or interact with its model in any way unless you explicitly tell it to. So let's roll up our sleeves and write some display logic.

We'll start with a view class for our Card model. All it needs to do is render the model into markup and save changes in the description and due date fields to the model:

```
jQuery/src/card.coffee
class window.CardView extends Backbone.View
  render: ->
    html = JST['templates/card']
      description: @model.get('description')
      dueDate: @model.get('due-date')

    @$el.html html
    @

  events:
    'change [name=card-description]': 'descriptionChangeHandler'
    'change [name=due-date]': 'dueDateChangeHandler'

  descriptionChangeHandler: (e) ->
    @model.save 'description', $(e.currentTarget).val()
    return

  dueDateChangeHandler: (e) ->
    @model.save 'due-date', $(e.currentTarget).val()
    return
```

Let's walk through the render method: when we instantiate the view, we pass in an options hash, and Backbone automatically sets model and $el as properties when passed. @model is a Card instance, and @$el is a jQuery object that's wrapped around the HTML element that the view is in charge of. For CardView, that's going to be a div with the card class. After putting the HTML from the template in the DOM, the method returns the view to allow chaining, for example cardView = new CardView(options).render().

render alone would be all we need if this view were unidirectional, simply allowing the data in the card model to be displayed. But we want it to be bidirectional, allowing the card model to be manipulated. So we define an events hash, which Backbone uses to listen for DOM events and send them to handlers. The hash keys are of the form "<selector> <event type>", and the values are the names of class methods. Using names rather than references to the methods themselves may seem strange, but Backbone has to call the methods in the context of the view object. A call to view[methodName](e) does that nicely, whereas method(e) would work only if method were bound to view.

The two handlers pull the value from the DOM element and pass it the model's save method. The save method is very powerful: it not only changes the attribute on the model (as the set method would), it also syncs the model to the server (or, for now, localStorage).

Next up, ColumnView:

jQuery/src/column.coffee

```coffee
class window.ColumnView extends Backbone.View

  initialize: (options) ->
    @cardViews = []
    @listenTo @model.get('cards'), 'add remove', =>
      @model.save()
      @render()
    super

  render: ->
    html = JST['templates/column']
      name: @model.get('name')
      cards: @model.get('cards').toJSON()

    @$el.html html

    @cardViews = @model.get('cards').map (card) =>
      cardView = new window.CardView(model: card)
      cardView.setElement @$("[data-card-id=#{card.get('id')}]")
      cardView.render()
      cardView
    @

  events:
    'change [name=column-name]': 'nameChangeHandler'
    'click [name=add-card]': 'addCardClickHandler'

  nameChangeHandler: (e) ->
    @model.save 'name', $(e.currentTarget).val()
    return

  addCardClickHandler: (e) ->
    newCard = new window.Card({}, {parse: true})
    newCard.save()
    @model.get('cards').add(newCard)
    return
```

Backbone calls initialize whenever a class is instantiated. We're using it here to declare an initially empty array of card views and to attach an event listener to our column's collection of cards, so that we re-render the entire column every time a card is added or removed. This approach is a bit inefficient, since it re-renders all of the cards that were in the collection before the event, but we can optimize later if necessary (using those cardViews).

Note that the default implementation of initialize is a no-op and the return value is ignored, so ending our implementation with super is unnecessary. However, it gives us some leeway when refactoring. If we changed ColumnView in the future to extend a subclass of Backbone.View, we'd almost certainly want to call that subclass's initialize from ColumnView's.

The render method here has a couple of wrinkles that weren't in CardView's. First, we have to do some minor data transformation: we're storing the column's cards as a CardCollection in the Column model, and Eco doesn't understand Backbone collections. Instead, we need to pass in an array containing our card data, which is exactly what a collection's toJSON method gives us. Second, after rendering the column template we have to create a CardView for each card, give it the DOM element we've just created for it, and tell it to render. Otherwise, we'd just have a column full of card placeholders.

In addition to a name change handler that works just like the input handlers in CardView, the column view has a click handler for the New Card button. When clicked, it appends a new card with a unique ID to both allCards and the column's collection. That will trigger an add event on the column's collection, which will re-render the column, thanks to the listener we attached in initialize.

Finally, we have BoardView, which is very similar to ColumnView:

```
jQuery/src/board.coffee
class window.BoardView extends Backbone.View
  initialize: (options) ->
    @listenTo @model.get('columns'), 'add remove', =>
      @model.save()
      @render()
    super

  render: ->
    html = JST['templates/board']
      name: @model.get('name')
      columns: @model.get('columns').toJSON()

    @$el.html html

    @model.get('columns').forEach (column) =>
```

```
    columnView = new window.ColumnView(model: column)
    columnView.setElement @$("[data-column-id=#{column.get('id')}]")
    columnView.render()
    columnView
  @

events:
  'change [name=board-name]': 'nameChangeHandler'
  'click [name=add-column]': 'addColumnClickHandler'

nameChangeHandler: (e) ->
  @model.save 'name', $(e.currentTarget).val()
  return

addColumnClickHandler: (e) ->
  newColumn = new window.Column({}, {parse: true})
  newColumn.save()
  @model.get('columns').add(newColumn)
  return
```

Finishing Touches

We have our templates, our models, and our views. All that's left is a tiny bit of initialization logic!

First, we need some initial data to put in localStorage if none exists. Because we didn't provide a way to create new boards, it's essential that we start with one:

```
jQuery/src/data.coffee
localStorage.boards ?= JSON.stringify([
  {
    id: 1
    name: 'New Board'
  }
])
localStorage.columns ?= JSON.stringify([])
localStorage.cards ?= JSON.stringify([])
```

If, after mucking around, you want to restore this blank slate, open up the browser console and run localStorage.clear().

And finally, we need to initialize a BoardView:

```
jQuery/src/application.coffee
# Wait for the DOM to be ready
$ ->
  # Fetch all boards and display the last (only) one
  board = window.allBoards.last()
  $board = $("<div class='board' data-board-id='#{board.get('id')}'></div>")
```

```
$('body').append $board
boardView = new window.BoardView(
  model: board
  el: $board
).render()
return
```

BoardView will take care of the rest, creating and rendering all of the subviews we may need.

And with that, we're finally ready to run CoffeeTasks. Just open index.html in your browser of choice, and you'll be greeted with a fully functional task list app with localStorage persistence! Of course, it looks a lot better with a few basic styles:

jQuery/css/style.css
```css
/* Use border-box sizing for all elements */
* {
  box-sizing: border-box;
}

/* Make <body> occupy the full height of the window */
html, body {
  height: 100%;
}

/* The current board should cover the whole page */
.board {
  height: 100%;
  padding: 16px;
  background: #ccc;
}

/* The name of the board should go across the top of the page */
input[name=board-name] {
  font-size: 24px;
  width: 100%;
  height: 34px;
}

/* The column container should use all remaining board space */
.column-container {
  position: absolute;
  top: 62px; /* board padding-top + board-name + margin */
  bottom: 16px;
}

/* Each column should be fixed-width and use all available height */
.column {
  position: relative;
```

```
  display: inline-block;
  width: 300px;
  height: 100%;
  margin-right: 8px;
  padding: 8px;
  background: #999;
}

/* The "Add column" button should appear where the new column would go */
button[name=add-column] {
  display: inline-block;
  height: 23px;
  vertical-align: top;
}

/* The name of the column should go across the top of the column */
input[name=column-name] {
  font-size: 18px;
  width: 100%;
}

/* The card container should use all remaining column space */
.card-container {
  position: absolute;
  top: 40px; /* column padding-top + column-name + margin */
  width: 100%;
}

/* Each card should use the card-container's width and stack vertically */
.card {
  margin-right: 16px; /* padding-left + padding-right */
  margin-bottom: 8px;
  padding: 8px;

  background: #ccc;
}

/* Clearfix to ensure that we provide enough height for floated content */
.card::after {
  display: table;
  clear: both;
  content: '';
}

/* Card descriptions should be full-width (height is determined by rows) */
textarea[name=card-description] {
  width: 100%;
}

/* Each card's due date should be flush right */
```

```
.due-date-label {
  float: right;
}

/* There should be some space between the due date and its description */
input[name=due-date] {
  margin-left: 8px;
}

/* The "Add card" button should have fixed height */
button[name=add-card] {
  height: 23px;
}
```

With those in place, you'll have something minimalist but functional. True, it won't win any design awards, but it's a working web application.

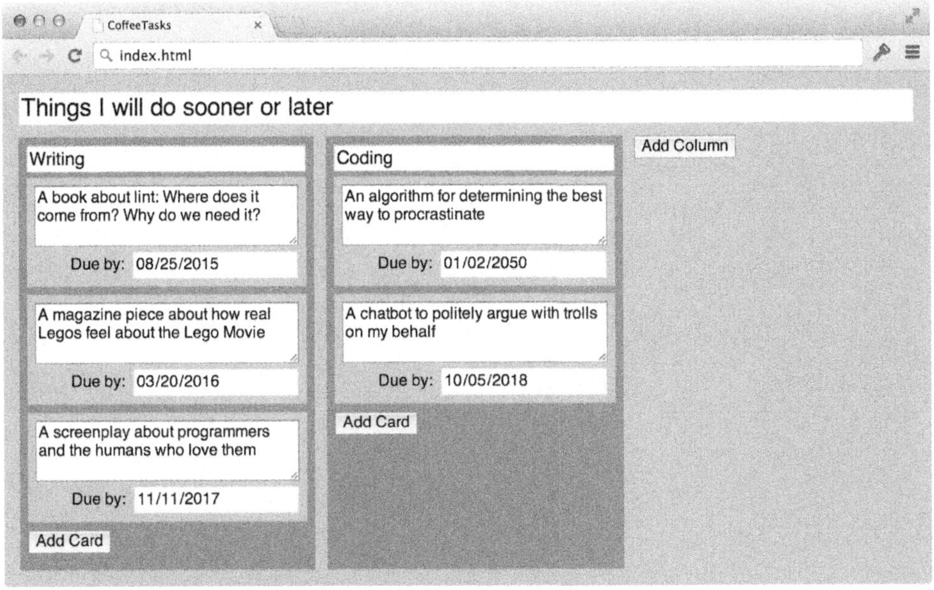

Figure 1—My own personal to-do list, organized in CoffeeTasks

Tasks That Last

In this chapter, we created a perfectly functional task manager—for one person. Because our data is tucked away in localStorage, there's no way to share it with anyone else—or with other devices, for that matter. In the next chapter, we'll take the front-end code that we've built here and give it a back end that allows our data to persist outside of the browser.

## CHAPTER 6

Web Servers with Node and Express

Running JavaScript on the server has long been a dream of web developers. Rather than switching back and forth between a client-side language and a server-side language, a developer using a JavaScript-powered server would need to be fluent only in that lingua franca of web apps—or in a dialect such as CoffeeScript.

Now that dream is finally a reality. In this chapter, we'll take a brief tour of Node, the preeminent environment for running JavaScript outside of the browser. Then we'll figure out just what an "evented architecture" is, with its implications for both server performance and our sanity. Finally, we'll create a Node back end for our project from the previous chapter, allowing us to persist our task cards in a proper database.

What Is Node?

Node (also called Node.js in contexts where the term "Node" might be ambiguous) is a JavaScript runtime environment powered by V8, the engine used by Google's Chrome browser. While browsers provide a JavaScript environment with an API that allows code to interact with a web page, the Node API gives JavaScript access to the underlying operating system. That means that scripts running in Node can read and write files, spawn processes, and bind to TCP ports. In fact, any functionality that can be accessed by a C program can be added to Node via addons.[1]

But the most exciting thing about Node isn't the technology, it's the community. Node developers have accomplished amazing feats since Node's debut in early 2009, building a rich ecosystem of open-source packages and using Node in production at high-profile companies such as PayPal, LinkedIn, and

---

1. http://nodejs.org/api/addons.html

Uber. To see some of the cool mini-projects the community has built, look no further than the Node Knockout, an annual competition to develop the best Node app in forty-eight hours.[2]

Node also has the best package manager on the planet, npm.[3] Although originally started independently, npm was quickly embraced as an official accompaniment to Node, and the two projects are now developed in tandem to complement each other. I like npm so much that I wrote a (short) book about it: *The npm Book*.[4] You'll get a taste of npm as we build this chapter's project.

Writing Node Modules

In the browser, isolating scripts is a pain. Ultimately, every variable a script defines is either scoped in a function or attached to the global object, called window. Expressing dependencies from one script on another is a pain, too. How many times have you written if (window.x) ...? These problems are addressed by the proposed standard for ES6 modules, but it will take years before browser support is widespread.

Thankfully, Node has its own solution to this problem. Every file is its own module with isolated variable scope. There is a global object, simply called global (more semantic than window, wouldn't you agree?), but it's rarely used. Instead, each module attaches data it wants to share to a special object called exports. When a script wants to load a module as a dependency, it uses Node's require function, passing in a partial file path. (More details on that in a moment.) Here's a simple example:

```
# strings.js
exports.hello = 'Hello, Node modules!';

# main.js
var strings = require('./strings');
console.log(strings.hello);

$ node main.js
Hello, Node modules!
```

When Node came across the function call require('./strings'), it blocked execution (a rare thing in Node) while it looked for any of the following in the same directory as main.js, in this order:

---

2.   http://nodeknockout.com/
3.   https://www.npmjs.org/
4.   https://leanpub.com/npm

1. strings.js (a JavaScript module)

2. strings.json (a JSON data file)

3. strings.node (a native addon)

4. A directory named strings with a file named index.js, index.json, or index.node (or a different file specified as "main" by a package.json in that directory)

In our example, of course, Node didn't have to look very far. It found strings.js, executed it, and returned the object corresponding to exports in strings.js from the require function in main.js.

When require is used with a nonrelative path, it looks for a file with that name in the directory where npm installs packages—or, more accurately, a hierarchy of directories, all named node_modules. It starts with ./node_modules, then ../node_modules, and so on until it gets down to /node_modules. (None of these directories has to exist, of course. Node simply skips the ones that don't.) Finally, it looks in a handful of global locations, although using global modules is discouraged. I mentioned some of the potential problems with global npm modules in *Building the Project with Grunt*, on page 50.

The rules for using require with a relative path combine beautifully with the node_modules hierarchy: when you npm install coffee-script, you get a node_modules/coffee-script directory with a package.json that points to the "main" JavaScript file that defines the API for the CoffeeScript compiler. That package.json also lists the project's own dependencies, which npm installs in node_modules/coffee-script/node_modules. Those, in turn, can have their own dependencies. But you don't have to worry about any of that from the root project: require('coffee-script') just works. And that's why npm is the best package manager on the planet.

You may be asking: "Okay, but how do I load a CoffeeScript file?" That's a reasonable question that's been an area of surprising controversy in Node-land. Early on, Node offered the ability to register extensions to require. After registering the .coffee file extension, you could write require('./script.coffee'), and Node would know to pass that file into the CoffeeScript compiler before executing it. However, the JavaScript purists disliked this feature, and it is now marked as deprecated. No big deal: compiling CoffeeScript before runtime is perfectly sensible. It allows us to deal with compile-time bugs and runtime bugs separately. With the project setup we'll create in the next section, we'll enjoy automatic recompilation, plus source maps for debugging. Who could ask for more?

Compiling a Node Project with Grunt

In the previous chapter, we used Grunt to compile our CoffeeScript files into JavaScript (and source maps) to be served to the browser. For this chapter's project, we'll have two kinds of CoffeeScript files: files that define JavaScript to be sent to the browser, and files that should be run locally in Node. So we'll keep them in two separate directories, /assets and /src. We'll use our Node server to serve our compiled assets to the browser. Any time any of our files change, we'll restart the Node server to ensure that it reflects our changes.

We'll keep our assets that don't have to be compiled (our CSS and HTML files, as well as the external JS we'll install through Bower) in the assets directory as well, and copy them into /lib with everything else we would need to deploy our project (except for the third-party packages in /node_modules). To do that, we'll use another Grunt plugin, grunt-contrib-copy.[5]

To manage our local Node server, we'll use the grunt-nodemon[6] plugin, which wraps around the excellent nodemon.[7] nodemon watches files and restarts our Node server.

One wrinkle: both grunt-contrib-watch (which we'll be using to automatically recompile our project when source files change, as in the previous chapter) and grunt-nodemon keep running indefinitely, and Grunt tasks normally run in a one-at-a-time fashion. To run them at the same time, we need to use yet another plugin, grunt-concurrent.[8]

If you think this sounds quite complicated, well, you're right. Setting up the perfect Grunt configuration for a project can take quite a bit of work, because the possibilities for custom tailoring are endless. But once it's set up, the dividends (compared to compiling manually) are enormous.

As in the last chapter, let's start by setting up our project directory:

```
$ mkdir coffee-tasks
$ cd coffee-tasks
$ npm init
```

And now let's install Grunt and the plugins we need, including the ones from the previous chapter:

---

5.   https://github.com/gruntjs/grunt-contrib-copy
6.   https://github.com/ChrisWren/grunt-nodemon
7.   https://github.com/remy/nodemon
8.   https://github.com/sindresorhus/grunt-concurrent

```
$ npm install -g grunt-cli
$ npm install --save-dev grunt
$ npm install --save-dev grunt-eco
$ npm install --save-dev grunt-concurrent
$ npm install --save-dev grunt-contrib-watch
$ npm install --save-dev grunt-contrib-copy
$ npm install --save-dev grunt-contrib-coffee
$ npm install --save-dev grunt-nodemon
```

Whew! Okay, that's all set. Now here's our Gruntfile:

Node/Gruntfile.coffee
```
module.exports = (grunt) ->
  grunt.loadNpmTasks('grunt-eco')
  grunt.loadNpmTasks('grunt-concurrent')
  grunt.loadNpmTasks('grunt-contrib-watch')
  grunt.loadNpmTasks('grunt-contrib-copy')
  grunt.loadNpmTasks('grunt-contrib-coffee')
  grunt.loadNpmTasks('grunt-nodemon')

  grunt.initConfig
    watch:
      coffeeAssets:
        files: 'assets/coffee/*.coffee'
        tasks: ['coffee:compileAssets']
      coffeeServer:
        files: 'src/*.coffee'
        tasks: ['coffee:compileServer']
      eco:
        files: 'assets/templates/*.eco'
        tasks: ['eco:compile']
      css:
        files: 'assets/css/*.css'
        tasks: ['copy:css']
      html:
        files: 'assets/html/*.html'
        tasks: ['copy:html']

    coffee:
      compileAssets:
        expand: true
        flatten: true
        options:
          sourceMap: true
        cwd: 'assets/coffee/'
        src: ['*.coffee']
        dest: 'lib/public/js/'
        ext: '.js'
      compileServer:
        expand: true
        flatten: true
```

```
    options:
      sourceMap: true
    cwd: 'src/'
    src: ['*.coffee']
    dest: 'lib/'
    ext: '.js'

eco:
  compile:
    options:
      basePath: 'assets'
    src: 'assets/templates/*.eco'
    dest: 'lib/public/js/templates.js'

copy:
  css:
    files: [{
      expand: true
      cwd: 'assets/css/'
      src: ['*.css']
      dest: 'lib/public/css/'
    }]
  html:
    files: [{
      expand: true
      cwd: 'assets/html/'
      src: ['*.html']
      dest: 'lib/public/'
    }]
  bower:
    files: [{
      expand: true
      flatten: true
      cwd: 'bower_components/'
      src: [
        'jquery/dist/jquery.js'
        'underscore/underscore.js'
        'backbone/backbone.js'
      ]
      dest: 'lib/public/js/'
    }]

nodemon:
  dev:
    script: 'lib/server.js'
    watch: 'lib'
    ext: '*'
    options:
      nodeArgs: ['--debug']
```

```
    concurrent:
      dev:
        tasks: ['nodemon', 'watch']
        options:
          logConcurrentOutput: true

  grunt.registerTask('build', ['coffee', 'eco', 'copy'])
  grunt.registerTask('default', ['build', 'concurrent'])
```

It's a lot to take in, but in practice it should feel pretty straightforward: you'll be editing files in /src (for the server) and /assets (for the front end), all of which will go into /lib. The root of /lib is reserved for the files that make up our Node server, while the contents of /lib/public will be directly available to the browser. This new directory structure allows us to simplify our index.html nicely:

Node/assets/html/index.html
```html
<!DOCTYPE html>
<html>
<head>
  <title>CoffeeTasks</title>

  <!-- Libraries -->
  <script src="js/jquery.js"></script>
  <script src="js/underscore.js"></script>
  <script src="js/backbone.js"></script>

  <!-- Templates -->
  <script src="js/templates.js"></script>

  <!-- Backbone models/views -->
  <script src="js/card.js"></script>
  <script src="js/column.js"></script>
  <script src="js/board.js"></script>

  <!-- Application core -->
  <script src="js/application.js"></script>

  <!-- Stylesheets -->
  <link rel="stylesheet" href="css/normalize.css">
  <link rel="stylesheet" href="css/style.css">
</head>
<body>
  <!-- All content is rendered client-side -->
</body>
</html>
```

In the next section, we'll get our server up and running.

Creating a Web Server with Express and NeDB

Node was built from the ground up to be an ideal runtime for high-capacity servers. As a result, the HTTP functions it comes with out of the box are thin abstractions over the TCP layer that provide streams of data that can be handled as rapidly as the packets arrive.

Of course, for most applications, stream-based functionality is overkill. We're perfectly happy reading the whole request before we decide to handle it and then sending a complete response. Also, we want to be able to think in terms of individual routes such as /moon-unit-alpha/ and /moon-unit-zappa/, rather than parsing every request's headers ourselves. These are basic abstractions that all Node web frameworks provide. Of these frameworks, the most popular is called Express.[9]

We need to install Express with npm:

```
$ npm install --save express
```

Once that's done, starting an Express server is easy:

Node/src/server.coffee
```
express = require 'express'
app = express()

# Start our Express server
port = process.env.PORT or 8520
app.listen port, ->
  console.log "Now listening on port #{port}"
```

With that, we have a fully operational web server, faithfully responding to every request with a 404 Not Found. We can make this server a whole lot more useful by telling it that it can serve all of the files in the public subdirectory of the directory server.js is in:

Node/src/server.coffee
```
app.use(express.static("#{__dirname}/public"))
```

Our server is now half-finished! If you run it and connect to http://localhost:8520 in your browser, the server will try to serve public/index.html. We'll set up our public files in the next section. But first, let's finish our server by implementing a database layer and a RESTful API for our project's data.

Which database to choose? There are countless high-quality open-source database projects these days. Debating SQL vs. NoSQL is all the rage (and

---

9. http://expressjs.com/

drives many developers to rage), and choosing the right database to ensure a project's future scalability is a nail-biting decision. Luckily, I'm writing a book about CoffeeScript, so I don't have to make any such decision. Instead, I'm going to pick the simplest option: NeDB.[10] NeDB (Node Embedded Database) is a document store (similar to MongoDB) with no external dependencies. Guess how you install it? That's right:

```
$ npm install --save nedb
```

We'll tell NeDB to store our objects in three files, one for each of our collections (mirroring the schema that we used in localStorage in the previous chapter). We'll also tell NeDB to index objects in each collection by their id property. This speeds up queries and, more importantly, ensures that objects remain uniquely identifiable by id:

Node/src/server.coffee
```
Datastore = require('nedb')
db = {}
['boards', 'columns', 'cards'].forEach (collectionKey) =>
  db[collectionKey] = new Datastore
    filename: "#{__dirname}/#{collectionKey}.db"
    autoload: true

  db[collectionKey].ensureIndex {fieldName: 'id', unique: true}
  return
```

Note the autoload option, which tells NeDB to buffer any commands it receives until it has opened the file on disk (or created the file if it didn't already exist).

This seems like a good place to create our initial data:

Node/src/server.coffee
```
# Set the initial board state if none already exists
db.boards.insert({
  id: 1
  name: 'New Board'
})
```

If a board with id: 1 already exists, NeDB will ignore the insertion attempt.

All we need to do now is wire up some API endpoints. First, let's install and use a convenient Express middleware that automatically parses JSON from POST and PUT request bodies:

```
$ npm install --save body-parser
```

---

10. https://github.com/louischatriot/nedb

Node/src/server.coffee

```coffee
bodyParser = require('body-parser')
app.use(bodyParser.json())
```

Now for the endpoint definitions themselves. For our minimal RESTful API, we need a way to fetch whole collections (GET), a way to insert a new object into a collection (POST), and a way to update an existing object (PUT):

Node/src/server.coffee

```coffee
['boards', 'columns', 'cards'].forEach (collectionKey) =>

  # Endpoint to fetch the entire collection
  app.get "/#{collectionKey}", (req, res) =>
    db[collectionKey].find {}, (err, collection) =>
      throw err if err
      res.send(collection)
      return

  # Endpoint to add a new object to the collection (assigns id)
  app.post "/#{collectionKey}", (req, res) =>
    object = req.body
    db[collectionKey].count {}, (err, count) =>
      throw err if err
      object.id = count + 1
      db[collectionKey].insert object, (err) =>
        throw err if err
        res.send(object)
        return

  # Endpoint to update an existing object in the collection
  app.put "/#{collectionKey}/:id", (req, res) =>
    query = {id: +req.params.id}
    object = req.body
    options = {}
    db[collectionKey].update query, object, options, (err) =>
      throw err if err
      res.send(object)
      return
```

Simple, isn't it? Document stores are a pleasure to work with! Of course, in a production application, we'd want to add a number of additional steps to these endpoints. We'd want to verify that the requester has access. We'd want to perform schema validation to prevent irregular objects from populating the database. We'd want to enforce storage limits and throttle requests to prevent the user from overwhelming our service. But for this project, I'm content to leave these elegant little endpoints alone.

One more thing: we'll have an easier time debugging if we take advantage of the source maps we've compiled. Node doesn't do this out of the box. Instead, we need to install the source-map-support package and run while we're in development mode:

```
$ npm install --save source-map-support
```

Node/src/server.coffee
```
# Read environment configuration
env = process.env.NODE_ENV or 'development'

# In development mode, enable source map support
if env is 'development'
  require('source-map-support').install()
```

In the next section, we'll update our front-end code from the previous chapter to take advantage of this newly created API.

Using a RESTful API in Backbone

In the previous chapter, we created a self-contained, in-browser web application using localStorage to persist data. Now we have a server set up to sync that data to disk instead, allowing our app to be used in any browser on potentially any machine. All we have to do is adapt our code.

We need all of the same external dependencies as in the previous chapter, so let's start by installing the same Bower modules as before:

```
$ bower init
$ bower install --save jquery
$ bower install --save backbone
```

Now on to our Backbone models and collections. We no longer need the initial data or the Backbone.sync shim from the previous chapter. All we need to do to tell Backbone how to talk to our RESTful API is attach a url value to each collection and model. Here's how our collection definitions look with that addition:

Node/assets/coffee/board.coffee
```
class window.BoardCollection extends Backbone.Collection
  model: Board
  url: '/boards'
```

Node/assets/coffee/column.coffee
```
class window.ColumnCollection extends Backbone.Collection
  model: Column
  url: '/columns'
```

Node/assets/coffee/card.coffee
```
class window.CardCollection extends Backbone.Collection
  model: Card
  url: '/cards'
```

When we call the fetch method on a collection, Backbone will make a GET request to that URL. Additionally, when we call save on a model, Backbone cleverly infers the URL to POST or PUT to based on the URL of the collection that the model belongs to. So there's no need to modify our models at all.

We need to make only a few more adjustments. In the localStorage-based version of the project, we were able to synchronously load all of our data. Now any action we perform is asynchronous. The leap from synchronous operations to asynchronous ones has many implications in a web application, and in fact I've devoted an entire book to the subject.[11]

The first problem is that we need to fetch the data for our three collections and parse it in a specific order: first cards, then columns, then boards. This is because our column models reference card models, and board models reference column models. So how do we do this without waiting for three sequential requests?

The answer is to make the requests in parallel and then parse the data in sequence. We can do this by telling our collections to fetch the data without parsing it. Each fetch will return a jQuery promise representing the Ajax request, so we can use jQuery's $.when to execute a callback only after all three requests have been completed. Each argument passed to the callback will consist of an array of the arguments that would be passed to that Ajax request's success handler. Of those, we care about only the first argument, the data. Here's the code:

```
Node/assets/coffee/application.coffee
# Fetch all card, column, and board data in parallel, then parse in sequence
fetchInitialData = $.when(
  new window.CardCollection().fetch(parse: false)
  new window.ColumnCollection().fetch(parse: false)
  new window.BoardCollection().fetch(parse: false)
)

fetchInitialData.then ([cardData], [columnData], [boardData]) =>
  options = {parse: true}
  window.allCards = new window.CardCollection(cardData, options)
  window.allColumns = new window.ColumnCollection(columnData, options)
  window.allBoards = new window.BoardCollection(boardData, options)
  renderBoard()
  return

renderBoard = =>
  # Display the last board as the page
```

---

11. https://pragprog.com/book/tbajs/async-javascript

```
board = window.allBoards.last()
$board = $("<div class='board' data-board-id='#{board.get('id')}'></div>")
$('body').append $board
boardView = new window.BoardView(
  model: board
  el: $board
).render()
```

The second problem is that we need to save new cards and columns in two places (the new object and the existing object that references it), and once again, order matters, because the new object's ID is assigned by the server—there's no way to save a reference until after the new object has been saved. So when we add a new card or column, we have to take these two steps in sequence:

Node/assets/coffee/board.coffee
```
addColumnClickHandler: (e) ->
  newColumn = new window.Column({}, {parse: true})
  allColumns.add(newColumn)
  newColumn.save().then =>
    @model.get('columns').add(newColumn)
    @model.save()
    @render()
    return
  return
```

Node/assets/coffee/column.coffee
```
addCardClickHandler: (e) ->
  newCard = new window.Card({}, {parse: true})
  allCards.add(newCard)
  newCard.save().then =>
    @model.get('cards').add(newCard)
    @model.save()
    @render()
    return
  return
```

And that does it! With those alterations, our Backbone application can now read from and write to our Node API. Open up http://localhost:8520 in your browser and behold the glory of a genuine web application!

A Brief Encounter with Node

Throughout the book, we've used Node in the background as the runtime environment for the CoffeeScript compiler. This chapter provided a very short introduction to Node in the capacity it's best known for: as an environment for server applications. With a little help from Express, we were able to implement a complete web application server in less than one hundred lines of CoffeeScript code. Imagine what you could do with just a few more.

We were able to set up a very handy development workflow, thanks to Grunt and Nodemon. CoffeeScript for both the front end and the back end compiled automatically, complete with source maps. The Node server automatically restarted. Perhaps the only major omission was automated testing—the subject of the next chapter.

## CHAPTER 7

Testing with Intern

Much has been said about the difficulties of testing in JavaScript. It's not so much the language as what the language is primarily used for: building interactive applications on the Web. Rocket science is hard, but writing tests for rocket software is relatively easy, because you only need to test that it computes the correct trajectories. Conversely, it's easy to build a web application, but writing good tests—the kind that will find bugs before your users do—is a challenge.

Still, it's a challenge worth facing head-on. The JavaScript testing ecosystem is light years beyond where it was just a few years ago. Test frameworks of all kinds have proliferated. Build systems that run automated tests before deploying a new version of a script have become the norm.

In this chapter, we'll write tests for the project from the previous chapter. We'll start by testing the UI in isolation, using mock Ajax. Then we'll test the Node server in isolation. Together, these tests will run rapidly while ensuring that both ends of our application behave as expected. And we'll implement both layers of testing using a single framework, Intern.[1]

Getting Started with Intern

Intern is a full-featured JavaScript test framework developed by the fine folks at SitePen. While there are other excellent options out there (most notably Mocha[2]), Intern stands out as a natural choice for testing CoffeeScript because it includes full support for source maps.

1. http://theintern.io/
2. http://mochajs.org/

Before we begin, make a copy of the project from the previous chapter in a new directory. Now let's install Intern as a development dependency and add a tests directory:

```
$ npm install --save-dev intern
$ mkdir tests
```

Intern doesn't have out-of-the-box support for CoffeeScript, so we'll be compiling our test files with Grunt. To accommodate that, let's subdivide tests:

```
$ mkdir tests/src
$ mkdir tests/compiled
```

In the Grunt config from the previous chapter, we have two tasks in the coffee section: compileAssets and compileServer. Now we'll add a third, compileTests, which will compile everything from tests/src into tests/compiled while preserving the directory structure:

Testing/Gruntfile.coffee
```
compileTests:
  expand: true
  flatten: false
  options:
    sourceMap: true
  cwd: 'tests/src'
  src: ['**/*.coffee']
  dest: 'tests/compiled/'
  ext: '.js'
```

Now, to run Intern, at a minimum we need a config file (named intern by convention) and at least one test suite file. In the later sections of this chapter, we'll create a new subdirectory of tests/src for each type of testing we're doing. For now, we'll create a subdirectory with a trivial test suite so that we can say "hello" to Intern testing:

```
$ mkdir tests/src/hello
```

Then we'll add a config file to our new directory:

Testing/tests/src/hello/intern.coffee
```
define
  suites: [
    'tests/compiled/hello/alwaysTrue'
  ]
```

The config points to the path of our test suite. Or, rather, the path where it'll be compiled to by Grunt. (Intern can't run CoffeeScript directly.) Speaking of the test suite, here it is:

Testing/tests/src/hello/alwaysTrue.coffee
```
define [
    'intern!object'
    'intern/chai!assert'
], (registerSuite, assert) ->

  registerSuite
    name: 'example suite'
    'example test': ->
      assert.strictEqual true, true, 'true is true in CoffeeScript'
```

Intern includes out-of-the-box support for Grunt in the form of an aptly named task:

Testing/Gruntfile.coffee
```
grunt.loadNpmTasks('intern')
```

This makes it easy to tell Grunt how to run our tests:

Testing/Gruntfile.coffee
```
intern:
  hello:
    options:
      runType: 'client'
      config: 'tests/compiled/hello/intern'
      reporters: ['console']
```

Now all we have to do is compile and run:

```
$ grunt coffee:compileTests
Running "coffee:compileTests" (coffee) task
>> 2 files created.
>> 2 source map files created.

Done, without errors.

$ grunt intern:hello
>> PASS: main - example suite - example test (0ms)
>> 0/1 tests failed
>> 0/1 tests failed
```

Great! Now we have zero tests failing, which is Intern's cheerful way of saying that everything passed. (The repetition is because Intern reports that statistic for each test suite, and then the combined total for all test suites.)

For convenience, let's define a single Grunt task to compile and run all of our tests:

Testing/Gruntfile.coffee
```
grunt.registerTask('test', ['coffee', 'intern'])
```

Now we can do all of our testing just by running grunt test. To make testing even easier for any future project collaborators (who we sincerely hope will run our test suites against any changes they make), let's tell npm that this is our project's standard test command. In the default package.json that npm creates, there's a section that looks like this:

```
"scripts": {
  "test": "echo \"Error: no test specified\" && exit 1"
}
```

This is npm's slightly passive-aggressive way of encouraging us to add tests to our project and to tell npm how to run those tests. Let's correct this omission:

```
"scripts": {
  "test": "grunt test"
}
```

And with that, we can run all of our project's tests with the command npm test, in accordance with Node conventions and good taste:

```
$ npm test
> grunt test

Running "coffee:compileTests" (coffee) task
>> 2 files created.
>> 2 source map files created.

Running "intern:hello" (intern) task
PASS: main - example suite - example test (0ms)
0/1 tests failed
0/1 tests failed
```

Now we're ready to write some real tests!

Mock-Testing Backbone with Sinon

To dip our toes into testing, we used Intern in Node mode. But to test the browser side of our application, we need to run our tests in a browser environment. (Well, "need" might be too strong a word. Let's just say that testing a browser-based application in a nonbrowser environment is less than ideal.) Yet we still want the ease and automatability of command-line testing. What to do?

The answer is Selenium, a project that allows browsers to be controlled from the command line. Selenium can run on virtually any system and talk to any major browser. In fact, several providers are available to sell Selenium as a service. Rather than running Selenium on your local machine, which would limit you to the browsers and the OS you have installed, you can run your tests in the cloud on every possible browser and OS combination you want to support.

For the remainder of this chapter, I'll be running my browser-based tests with a remote Selenium service called Sauce Labs.[3] They offer a fourteen-day free trial with no credit card required. In addition to versatility, running Selenium remotely is a lot less of a hassle. However, if you'd prefer not to use a remote testing provider, you can download Selenium Server for yourself.[4]

For our UI unit tests, let's create a new directory:

```
$ mkdir tests/src/ui_unit
```

And let's add a new task to our Grunt config. In addition to pointing to an Intern config file in the new directory (which we'll create momentarily), we specify runType: 'runner' instead of runType: 'client', meaning that the tests will run in a Selenium runner instead of a Node client:

Testing/Gruntfile.coffee
```
ui_unit:
  options:
    runType: 'runner'
    config: 'tests/compiled/ui_unit/intern'
    reporters: ['console']
```

Now let's create the Intern config for our new test directory, pointing at one test suite for each of our app's three Backbone entities:

Testing/tests/src/ui_unit/intern.coffee
```
define
  excludeInstrumentation: /^(?:tests|bower_components)\//
  loader:
    packages: [
      {name: 'sinon', location: 'bower_components/sinon/lib'}
      {name: 'jquery', location: 'bower_components/jquery/dist'}
      {name: 'underscore', location: 'bower_components/underscore'}
      {name: 'backbone', location: 'bower_components/backbone'}
      {name: 'app', location: 'assets/coffee'}
    ]
  suites: [
    'tests/compiled/ui_unit/board'
    'tests/compiled/ui_unit/column'
    'tests/compiled/ui_unit/card'
  ]
  environments: [
```

---

3. https://saucelabs.com/
4. http://docs.seleniumhq.org/download/

```
    {
      browserName: 'chrome'
      version: ['38']
      platform: ['Linux']
    }
  ]
  # Add your own tunnel here, e.g.
  # tunnel: 'SauceLabsTunnel'
  # tunnelOptions: {
  #   username: 'my-username'
  #   accessKey: 'ea961239-0c3c-c3ab-715c-99de41defaa8'
  # }
```

There's a lot more going on here than there was in our first Intern config. First of all, there's excludeInstrumentation. This regular expression tells Intern to ignore any scripts whose path contains tests or bower_components when computing code coverage statistics, ensuring that those statistics only pertain to our application code.

The packages map given to loader (referring to Intern's AMD module loader) tells it where to look for various scripts that need to be loaded in the test suites. I like to keep this information in the Intern config rather than having to repeat all of these paths across every test suite.

As in our first Intern config, suites points Intern to the test suites we'll be compiling.

Now here's where things get interesting: environments tells Intern what kind of virtual machine to request from our test environment provider (e.g. Sauce Labs). You can provide multiple environments here to run all of your tests in each of several browsers. For now, I'm keeping things simple by just requesting a recent version of Chrome under Linux.

Finally, you'll need to un-comment the tunnel and tunnelOptions lines and enter your test environment provider credentials, unless you're running Selenium locally. For more information on configuring Intern, the docs are in the wiki: https://github.com/theintern/intern/wiki/Configuring-Intern

Now to write our first unit test! Let's start with our simplest entity, Card. The Card model has no functionality of its own, beyond what it gets by subclassing Backbone.Model. CardCollection, however, has to talk to the server to fetch data. So we should write a test to confirm that the collection populates as expected after we call fetch.

We could run a remote server for the test browser to talk to, but if we did that, our tests could fail for any number of reasons (server failure, network failure, server and browser code out of sync). We want to be sure that test failures indicate a problem with our browser code only. So instead, we'll use "mock" Ajax: any time our app would send an Ajax request, we'll intercept it and dictate the response in our test code. To do that, we'll use a library called Sinon.[5]

Let's start by installing Sinon with Bower:

```
$ bower install --save-dev sinon
```

We need to tell Intern to load Sinon into the browser. Intern uses an AMD (Asynchronous Module Definition[6]) loader. The good news is that Sinon supports AMD. The bad news is that it supports it in an unusual way, where you have to individually load each part of Sinon you need. So, to avoid repeating all of those declarations across every test suite, let's create a utility file:

Testing/tests/src/ui_unit/utils/sinon.coffee
```
define [
  'intern/order!sinon/sinon'
  'intern/order!sinon/sinon/spy'
  'intern/order!sinon/sinon/call'
  'intern/order!sinon/sinon/behavior'
  'intern/order!sinon/sinon/stub'
  'intern/order!sinon/sinon/mock'
  'intern/order!sinon/sinon/collection'
  'intern/order!sinon/sinon/assert'
  'intern/order!sinon/sinon/sandbox'
  'intern/order!sinon/sinon/test'
  'intern/order!sinon/sinon/test_case'
  'intern/order!sinon/sinon/match'
  'intern/order!sinon/sinon/util/event'
  'intern/order!sinon/sinon/util/fake_xml_http_request'
], (sinon) ->

  sinon
```

Whew! As you can see, Sinon has quite a few features to offer. But what exactly do those strings mean?

Anything before a ! in an AMD loader string is a plugin name. That means that the plugin takes the module specified by the rest of the string and performs some operation on it. In this case, we're using the intern/order plugin. Its effect is very simple: it ensures that the referenced scripts run in the order we've specified. This is important for Sinon, because the later scripts try to attach objects to the global sinon object defined by the first script.

---

5. http://sinonjs.org/
6. https://github.com/amdjs/amdjs-api/blob/master/AMD.md

The sinon/ at the start of the module path proper points to the path that we referenced in our Intern config's packages section. The rest is just the path of a ..js file. We'll continue to use this idiom for every component we load from outside of Intern.

In our actual test module, we need to load not only Sinon, but also—and arguably more importantly—the entities we're testing. Also, since those entities rely on Backbone, we'll have to bring Backbone into the test. Backbone, in turn, expects Underscore and jQuery to be defined. So we bring all of those, using the intern/order plugin to preserve the order in which the modules need to be loaded into the browser:

Testing/tests/src/ui_unit/card.coffee
```coffee
define [
    'intern!object'
    'intern/chai!assert'
    './utils/sinon'
    'intern/order!jquery/jquery'
    'intern/order!underscore/underscore'
    'intern/order!backbone/backbone'
    'intern/order!app/card'
], (registerSuite, assert, sinon) ->
```

For our first real unit test, let's mock an empty response and confirm that the collection contains no cards:

Testing/tests/src/ui_unit/card.coffee
```coffee
fakeXHR = null
responseHeaders = {'Content-type': 'application/json'}

startFakeXHR = ->
  fakeXHR = sinon.useFakeXMLHttpRequest()
  fakeXHR.requests = []
  fakeXHR.onCreate = (req) ->
    fakeXHR.requests.push(req)

stopFakeXHR = ->
  fakeXHR.restore()

registerSuite
  name: 'CardCollection'

  'has no cards after empty response from /cards': ->
    startFakeXHR()
    cards = new window.CardCollection()

    fetchPromise = cards.fetch()
    assert.equal(requests[0].url, '/cards')
    requests[0].respond(200, responseHeaders, JSON.stringify([]))
```

```
# Return this promise so Intern knows when the test is over
fetchPromise.then =>
  assert.strictEqual cards.length, 0
  stopFakeXHR()
```

This bears some explaining. What's with startFakeXHR and stopFakeXHR? Well, when we call Sinon's useFakeXMLHttpRequest, we override the global XMLHttpRequest function. Unfortunately, Intern uses that same function to communicate with us! (We're running this test on a remote server, remember?) So we have to restore the browser's XHR functionality right away.

There's also the matter of timing. By default, Intern assumes that a test is done as soon as you return from it; it reports the result and moves on. But a fetch (even a mocked one) is asynchronous—the collection won't be populated until after the test function returns. So we have to return a promise representing the completion of the test. The one returned by fetch().then will do nicely. If you're not familiar with promises, Sandeep Panda has provided a good overview.[7]

And now let's mock a slightly more interesting response:

Testing/tests/src/ui_unit/card.coffee
```
'has 2 cards after 2-length response from /cards': ->
  startFakeXHR()
  cards = new window.CardCollection()

  fetchPromise = cards.fetch()
  assert.equal(requests[0].url, '/cards')
  requests[0].respond(200, responseHeaders, JSON.stringify([
    {id: '1', description: 'First'}
    {id: '2', description: 'Second'}
  ]))

  # Return this promise so Intern knows when the test is over
  fetchPromise.then =>
    assert.strictEqual cards.length, 2
    stopFakeXHR()
```

Excellent! Now if we just do the same for Column and Board, we'll have all of the parts of our front end that talk directly to the server covered. Speaking of the server...

---

7. http://www.sitepoint.com/overview-javascript-promises/

Mock-Testing a Node Server with Supertest

In the previous section, we tested each of our Backbone entities against a mock server, using Sinon to fake responses to each collection's HTTP requests. Now it's time to create the mirror image of those tests, testing that our server provides the correct response to a set of fake requests.

Before we start writing tests, though, we should refactor our server to make it test-friendly. As we wrote it originally, it would define an Express instance (called app) and then immediately start listening on a port. For testing, we don't want to actually open a TCP port. It's much easier to simulate our requests. So let's separate the code that defines app from the code that tells app to start listening:

Testing/src/app.coffee
```coffee
# Read environment configuration
env = process.env.NODE_ENV or 'development'

# In development mode, enable source map support
if env is 'development'
  require('source-map-support').install()

# Create an Express server instance
express = require 'express'
app = express()

app.use(express.static("#{__dirname}/public"))

Datastore = require('nedb')
db = {}
['boards', 'columns', 'cards'].forEach (collectionKey) =>
  db[collectionKey] = new Datastore
    filename: "#{__dirname}/#{collectionKey}.db"
    autoload: true

  db[collectionKey].ensureIndex {fieldName: 'id', unique: true}
  return

# Set the initial board state if none already exists
db.boards.insert({
  id: 1
  name: 'New Board'
})

bodyParser = require('body-parser')
app.use(bodyParser.json())

['boards', 'columns', 'cards'].forEach (collectionKey) =>
```

```
# Endpoint to fetch the entire collection
app.get "/#{collectionKey}", (req, res) =>
  db[collectionKey].find {}, (err, collection) =>
    throw err if err
    res.send(collection)
    return

# Endpoint to add a new object to the collection (assigns id)
app.post "/#{collectionKey}", (req, res) =>
  object = req.body
  db[collectionKey].count {}, (err, count) =>
    throw err if err
    object.id = count + 1
    db[collectionKey].insert object, (err) =>
      throw err if err
      res.send(object)
      return

# Endpoint to update an existing object in the collection
app.put "/#{collectionKey}/:id", (req, res) =>
  query = {id: +req.params.id}
  object = req.body
  options = {}
  db[collectionKey].update query, object, options, (err) =>
    throw err if err
    res.send(object)
    return
```

```
# Export the server instance
module.exports = app
```

Because this module just defines and exports app, it's now dual-purpose. We can require it and run assertions against it, or we can require it and call the listen method to start the server.

Now to write some Node tests. In the browser, we used Sinon to simulate Ajax requests. Here, we'll use Supertest[8] to simulate requests to our Node server. Let's start by installing Supertest as a dev dependency:

```
$ npm install --save-dev supertest
```

Now let's create a new folder for our new tests:

```
$ mkdir tests/src/node_unit
```

And a Gruntfile section, just like the one for our UI tests but with runType: 'client' (meaning "Node client") instead of runType: 'runner':

---

8. https://github.com/tj/supertest

Testing/Gruntfile.coffee
```coffee
node_unit:
  options:
    runType: 'client'
    config: 'tests/compiled/node_unit/intern'
    reporters: ['console']
```

For Node tests, we don't need anything like Selenium, so our Intern config will be much simpler:

Testing/tests/src/node_unit/intern.coffee
```coffee
define
  excludeInstrumentation: /^(?:tests|node_modules)\//
  suites: [
    'tests/compiled/node_unit/cardEndpoint'
  ]
```

(Notice that we've excluded node_modules from instrumentation here, since we aren't worried about how well our tests cover our third-party libraries.)

Our dependencies will be simpler as well. All we need is our basic testing libraries and the module that defines our Express instance:

Testing/tests/src/node_unit/cardEndpoint.coffee
```coffee
define [
    'intern!object'
    'intern/chai!assert'
    'intern/dojo/node!supertest'
    'intern/dojo/node!../../../lib/app'
], (registerSuite, assert, supertest, server) ->
```

Now for the test itself. At a minimum, we should make sure that the /cards endpoint yields a 200 response, while a request to a nonexistent endpoint yields a 404:

Testing/tests/src/node_unit/cardEndpoint.coffee
```coffee
registerSuite
  name: 'card endpoint'

  'request for cards yields a 200 response': ->
    supertest(server).get('/cards')
      .expect(200)
      .end (err, res) =>
        throw err if err

  'request for bad URL yields a 404 response': ->
    supertest(server).get('/adsfsfd')
      .expect(404)
      .end (err, res) =>
        throw err if err
```

We should, of course, write analogous tests for every endpoint our server provides, but this is a good starting point. Now to build our Node server and run our final batch of tests:

```
$ grunt build
$ grunt intern:node_unit
>> PASS: main - card endpoint - request for cards yields a 200 response (8ms)
>> PASS: main - card endpoint - request for bad URL yields a 404 response (1ms)
>> 0/2 tests failed
>> 0/2 tests failed
```

Closing Words

In this chapter, we've taken our simple project and added the basic tests needed to prevent regressions as our code is updated and new features are added. With unit tests on the front end that mock the back end and vice versa, we have the makings of a robust, maintainable, and lightning-fast set of tests.

And that's important, because it's not enough to just use CoffeeScript to build web applications faster. I think it behooves us, as CoffeeScript devs, to use that time we don't spend wrangling curly braces to make our apps better—to write web apps with useful features, great design, and solid engineering under it all. Our apps should be malleable in the face of change and tough in the face of attacks.

Congratulations on reaching the end of this book. I hope it's given you the knowledge and confidence you need to be a successful CoffeeScripter. Now go build something great.

Bibliography

[Hav11]   Marijn Haverbeke. *Eloquent JavaScript: A Modern Introduction to Program-mings*. No Starch Press, San Francisco, CA, 2011.

[Her12]   David Herman. *Effective JavaScript: 68 Specific Ways to Harness the Power of JavaScript*. Addison-Wesley Professional, Boston, MA, 2012.

[Hog14]   Brian P. Hogan. *Automate with Grunt: The Build Tool for JavaScript*. The Pragmatic Bookshelf, Raleigh, NC and Dallas, TX, 2014.

[Sei09]   Peter Seibel. *Coders at Work: Reflections on the Craft of Programming*. Apress, New York City, NY, 2009.

Index

The Modern Web

Get up to speed on the latest HTML, CSS, and JavaScript techniques.

HTML5 and CSS3 (2nd edition)

HTML5 and CSS3 are more than just buzzwords—
they're the foundation for today's web applications.
This book gets you up to speed on the HTML5 elements
and CSS3 features you can use right now in your current projects, with backwards compatible solutions
that ensure that you don't leave users of older browsers
behind. This new edition covers even more new features, including CSS animations, IndexedDB, and
client-side validations.

Brian P. Hogan
(300 pages) ISBN: 9781937785598. $38
https://pragprog.com/book/bhh52e

Async JavaScript

With the advent of HTML5, front-end MVC, and
Node.js, JavaScript is ubiquitous—and still messy.
This book will give you a solid foundation for managing
async tasks without losing your sanity in a tangle of
callbacks. It's a fast-paced guide to the most essential
techniques for dealing with async behavior, including
PubSub, evented models, and Promises. With these
tricks up your sleeve, you'll be better prepared to
manage the complexity of large web apps and deliver
responsive code.

Trevor Burnham
(104 pages) ISBN: 9781937785277. $17
https://pragprog.com/book/tbajs

Be Agile

Don't just "do" agile; you want to *be* agile. We'll show you how, for new code and old.

Your Code As a Crime Scene

Jack the Ripper and legacy codebases have more in common than you'd think. Inspired by forensic psychology methods, this book teaches you strategies to predict the future of your codebase, assess refactoring direction, and understand how your team influences the design. With its unique blend of forensic psychology and code analysis, this book arms you with the strategies you need, no matter what programming language you use.

Adam Tornhill
(190 pages) ISBN: 9781680500387. $36
https://pragprog.com/book/atcrime

The Nature of Software Development

You need to get value from your software project. You need it "free, now, and perfect." We can't get you there, but we can help you get to "cheaper, sooner, and better." This book leads you from the desire for value down to the specific activities that help good Agile projects deliver better software sooner, and at a lower cost. Using simple sketches and a few words, the author invites you to follow his path of learning and understanding from a half century of software development and from his engagement with Agile methods from their very beginning.

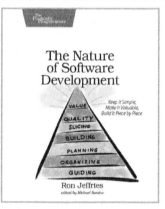

Ron Jeffries
(150 pages) ISBN: 9781941222379. $24
https://pragprog.com/book/rjnsd

Past and Present

To see where we're going, remember how we got here, and learn how to take a healthier approach to programming.

Fire in the Valley

In the 1970s, while their contemporaries were protesting the computer as a tool of dehumanization and oppression, a motley collection of college dropouts, hippies, and electronics fanatics were engaged in something much more subversive. Obsessed with the idea of getting computer power into their own hands, they launched from their garages a hobbyist movement that grew into an industry, and ultimately a social and technological revolution. What they did was invent the personal computer: not just a new device, but a watershed in the relationship between man and machine. This is their story.

Michael Swaine and Paul Freiberger
(424 pages) ISBN: 9781937785765. $34
https://pragprog.com/book/fsfire

The Healthy Programmer

To keep doing what you love, you need to maintain your own systems, not just the ones you write code for. Regular exercise and proper nutrition help you learn, remember, concentrate, and be creative—skills critical to doing your job well. Learn how to change your work habits, master exercises that make working at a computer more comfortable, and develop a plan to keep fit, healthy, and sharp for years to come.

This book is intended only as an informative guide for those wishing to know more about health issues. In no way is this book intended to replace, countermand, or conflict with the advice given to you by your own healthcare provider including Physician, Nurse Practitioner, Physician Assistant, Registered Dietician, and other licensed professionals.

Joe Kutner
(254 pages) ISBN: 9781937785314. $36
https://pragprog.com/book/jkthp

The Pragmatic Bookshelf

The Pragmatic Bookshelf features books written by developers for developers. The titles continue the well-known Pragmatic Programmer style and continue to garner awards and rave reviews. As development gets more and more difficult, the Pragmatic Programmers will be there with more titles and products to help you stay on top of your game.

Visit Us Online

This Book's Home Page
https://pragprog.com/book/tbcoffee2
Source code from this book, errata, and other resources. Come give us feedback, too!

Register for Updates
https://pragprog.com/updates
Be notified when updates and new books become available.

Join the Community
https://pragprog.com/community
Read our weblogs, join our online discussions, participate in our mailing list, interact with our wiki, and benefit from the experience of other Pragmatic Programmers.

New and Noteworthy
https://pragprog.com/news
Check out the latest pragmatic developments, new titles and other offerings.

Save on the eBook

Save on the eBook versions of this title. Owning the paper version of this book entitles you to purchase the electronic versions at a terrific discount.

PDFs are great for carrying around on your laptop—they are hyperlinked, have color, and are fully searchable. Most titles are also available for the iPhone and iPod touch, Amazon Kindle, and other popular e-book readers.

Buy now at *https://pragprog.com/coupon*

Contact Us

Online Orders:	*https://pragprog.com/catalog*
Customer Service:	*support@pragprog.com*
International Rights:	*translations@pragprog.com*
Academic Use:	*academic@pragprog.com*
Write for Us:	*http://write-for-us.pragprog.com*
Or Call:	+1 800-699-7764

CPSIA information can be obtained at www.ICGtesting.com
Printed in the USA
BVOW09s0847060215

386693BV00015B/245/P